100 Wok Dishes

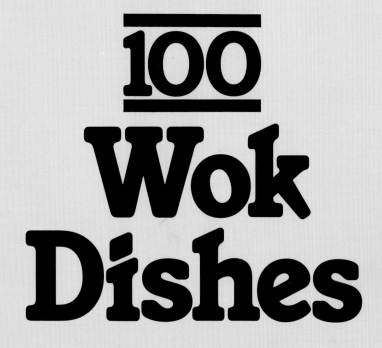

100
Wok
Dishes

Edited by
Barbara Croxford

HAMLYN

Contents

NOTES
Standard spoon measurements are used in all recipes
1 tablespoon = one 15 ml spoon
1 teaspoon = one 5 ml spoon
All spoon measures are level

Fresh herbs are used unless otherwise stated. If unobtainable, substitute a bouquet garni of the equivalent dried herbs, or use dried herbs instead but halve the quantities stated.
For all recipes, quantities are given in metric, imperial and American measures. Follow one set of measures only, because they are not interchangeable.

First published in 1983 by
Octopus Books Limited

This edition published in 1990 by
The Hamlyn Publishing Group Limited,
part of Reed International Books,
Michelin House, 81 Fulham Road,
London SW3 6RB

Copyright © 1983 Reed International Books Limited

Reprinted 1991, 1992

All rights reserved. No part of this publication
may be reproduced, stored in a retrieval system,
or transmitted, in any form or by any means, electronic,
mechanical, photocopying, recording, or otherwise,
without the permission of the publisher.

ISBN 0 600 56992 6

Produced by Mandarin Offset
Printed and bound in Hong Kong

Frontispiece: Honeyed Chicken (page 41)
(Photograph: Gale's Honey Bureau)

Introduction

Used in China for hundreds of years, the Chinese wok is ideal for preparing both oriental and western dishes. Although stir-frying is the most commonly used cooking method, you can also steam, braise, deep fry, simmer and shallow fry in the wok over gas or electric burners.

The unique shape of the wok heats fast and uses less fuel to maintain the temperature. Cooking over high heat for stir-frying conserves vitamins, flavour and colour. Meats are browned but remain juicy and tender; vegetables retain their fresh taste, and seafoods keep their delicate flavour.

After cooking a few stir-fried Chinese dishes in the wok, you will see that dishes like beef Stroganoff, ratatouille, scrambled eggs, risottos and many more can be cooked perfectly in your new cooking vessel.

Buying a wok

There are now many kinds of wok on the market, all very similar in shape but made of different metals and with varying finishes. For the best in cooking efficiency, choose a simple one made of rolled low-carbon steel. Most woks have two handles – the ones with wood covered handles are the best.

Some utensils are sold with the wok. Here is a list of useful, but not essential items: a perforated metal ring so that the wok sits securely on the stove; a domed metal lid for steaming, braising and cooking a whole chicken or duck; steaming rack; bamboo steamer (usually sold in a set of two tiers with one lid); spatula or *chan*; bamboo brush to clean wok; ladle; perforated spoon; strainer; Chinese cleaver.

Seasoning and caring for your wok

As woks are made from different metals and with varying finishes, do read the manufacturer's instructions carefully before use.

To season a steel wok, first wash well in hot soapy water to get rid of dust, industrial grime and machine oil. If necessary, remove coating of oil with a wire wool scourer. Rinse and dry.

Add 2 tablespoons oil to the clean wok, swirl this all round the sides. Heat for 2 to 3 minutes. Wipe out with kitchen paper towels and repeat the process. To make sure there is no metallic taste left, stir-fry a chopped onion in 2 tablespoons oil for several minutes, then discard.

After cooking a dish in the wok, do not scrub with a wire wool scourer or any abrasive material. If food sticks, soak the wok in hot water, then rub gently with a sponge or a bamboo brush. Dry well. Rub a lightly oiled paper towel over the inner surface of the wok. If it is necessary to use a wire wool scourer in the wok, the wok must then be reseasoned.

Hang your wok in the kitchen or store on an open shelf. Eventually, through repeated use, a dark brown film will develop. The wok is then properly seasoned.

General wok cooking instructions

It is best to use peanut oil for cooking in a wok as it has not a dominant flavour and cooks at high temperatures without smoking. Soya, sunflower seed, safflower and corn oil are excellent alternatives.

Prepare all ingredients before starting to cook as the wok cooks fast and efficiently, particularly when stir-frying. Meats are usually thinly sliced, cut into strips or minced (ground). Vegetables are finely chopped, thinly sliced, diced, shredded or cut into julienne (matchstick) strips. Some vegetables which need slightly longer cooking, such as celery and carrots can be sliced diagonally for faster cooking. The knife is held at an angle of 45 degrees when slicing.

Heat the wok first, add the oil and heat until just beginning to smoke. Carefully pick up the wok and swirl to coat the sides with oil.

Stir-frying: This is the tossing, flipping and turning over of food over high heat at speed so that all the surfaces of the food come into contact with the hot wok. Stir-fried food must be served immediately.

Steaming: food is placed in a shallow, heatproof dish on a steaming rack (or a suitable upturned plate, dish or saucer) in the wok, over simmering water – or the food is placed directly on the rack. The wok is covered with the lid and the steam cooks the food. Always ensure the water is simmering before placing the food on the rack.

Braising and simmering: the meat is browned in the oil in the wok. It is then removed and the vegetables are added to the wok and stir-fried. The meat is then replaced in the wok on the bed of vegetables. Liquid is added and the wok is covered. The food is simmered over a lower heat.

Deep frying: foods deep-fried in a wok are pleasantly crisp with no trace of greasiness. The temperature of the oil should be about 190°C/375°F before frying. The oil should be about 7.5-10 cm/3-4 inches deep.

Fish & Shellfish Dishes

Steamed Whole Fish

METRIC/IMPERIAL	AMERICAN
1 kg/2 lb sea bass or any whole fish, cleaned	2 lb sea bass or any whole fish, cleaned
2-3 slices pickled ginger or peeled root ginger, finely shredded	2-3 slices pickled ginger or peeled ginger root, finely shredded
1 tablespoon dry sherry	1 tablespoon dry sherry
1 tablespoon oil	1 tablespoon oil
1 jar Canton black bean stir-fry sauce	1 jar Canton black bean stir-fry sauce
4-5 spring onions, finely shredded	4-5 scallions, finely shredded
2 rashers back bacon, rinds removed and shredded	2 slices bacon, shredded

Rub the inside and outside of the fish with the ginger, sherry and oil. Leave for 15 minutes. Place the fish in a shallow heatproof dish (one which will fit in your wok), pour the black bean sauce along the length of the fish and rub in lightly. Sprinkle the spring onions (scallions) and bacon over the top.

Place on the steaming rack over simmering water. Cover with the lid and steam for 15 to 20 minutes or until the fish will flake easily.

From back: Braised Knuckle (Hock) of Pork (page 33); Lettuce in Oyster Sauce (page 56); Steamed Whole Fish; Beef Chow Mein (page 16), and lychees
(Photograph: J A Sharwood Co Ltd)

Mixed Seafood Chop Suey

METRIC/IMPERIAL	AMERICAN
2 tablespoons oil	2 tablespoons oil
1 large onion, sliced	1 large onion, sliced
3 slices root ginger, peeled and shredded	3 slices ginger root, peeled and shredded
3 rashers back bacon, rinds removed and cut into strips	3 slices Canadian bacon, cut into strips
300 ml/½ pint water	1¼ cups water
3 tablespoons soy sauce	3 tablespoons soy sauce
100 g/4 oz Chinese egg noodles	¼ lb Chinese egg noodles
350 g/12 oz cod fillet, cut into bite-size pieces	¾ lb cod or similar white fish fillet, cut into bite-size pieces
100 g/4 oz peeled prawns	⅔ cup shelled shrimp
1 × 150 g/5 oz can clams, drained	1 can (5 oz) clams, drained
freshly ground pepper	freshly ground pepper

Heat the oil in the wok. Add the onion, ginger and bacon and stir-fry for about 5 minutes or until tender. Add the water, soy sauce and noodles. Cook for 1 minute. Stir in the cod, prawns (shrimp), clams and pepper to taste. Cook for about 8 minutes or until the fish flakes easily when tested with a fork. Serve with lightly cooked broccoli.
Serves 4

Sweet and Sour Fish

METRIC/IMPERIAL	AMERICAN
1 kg/2 lb cod fillets, cut into bite-size pieces	2 lb cod or similar white fish fillets, cut into bite-size pieces
450 g/1 lb peeled prawns	1 lb shelled shrimp
cornflour	cornstarch
about 4 tablespoons oil	about ¼ cup oil
2 onions, thinly sliced	2 onions, thinly sliced
4 sticks celery, sliced diagonally	4 stalks celery, sliced diagonally
1 red pepper, cored, seeded and cut into thin strips	1 red pepper, seeded and cut into thin strips
½ bunch spring onions, sliced diagonally	½ bunch scallions, sliced diagonally
salt and freshly ground pepper	salt and freshly ground pepper
Marinade:	**Marinade:**
250 ml/8 fl oz chicken stock	1 cup chicken stock or broth
1 tablespoon tomato purée	1 tablespoon tomato paste
1 tablespoon soy sauce	1 tablespoon soy sauce
1 teaspoon ground ginger	1 teaspoon ground ginger
3 tablespoons white wine or water	3 tablespoons white wine or water

To make the marinade: mix together half the chicken stock, the tomato purée (paste), soy sauce, ginger and wine or water. Place the fish and prawns (shrimp) in this mixture and leave to marinate for 1 hour.

Drain all the fish and reserve the marinade. Toss the fish and prawns (shrimp) in cornflour (cornstarch) to coat. Heat about 3 tablespoons of the oil in the wok. Add the fish and prawns (shrimp) and stir-fry until golden brown. Remove and keep hot. Heat the remaining oil in the wok. Add the onions and fry until transparent. Add the celery, red pepper and spring onions (scallions) and stir-fry for 3 to 4 minutes.

Return the cooked fish and prawns (shrimp) with the reserved marinade, mixed with 2 teaspoons cornflour (cornstarch), the remaining stock and salt and pepper to taste. Bring to the boil, stirring constantly. Serve with rice, noodles or baked jacket potatoes.
Serves 6

Stir-Fried Seafood and Noodles

METRIC/IMPERIAL	AMERICAN
100 g/4 oz Chinese egg noodles	¼ lb Chinese egg noodles
2 tablespoons oil	2 tablespoons oil
5 spring onions, cut into 1 cm/½ inch pieces	5 scallions, cut into ½ inch pieces
2.5 cm/1 inch piece root ginger, peeled and thinly sliced	1 inch piece ginger root, peeled and thinly sliced
1 clove garlic, sliced	1 clove garlic, sliced
3 sticks celery, chopped	3 stalks celery, chopped
450 ml/¾ pint chicken stock	2 cups chicken stock or broth
2 tablespoons soy sauce	2 tablespoons soy sauce
1 tablespoon honey	1 tablespoon honey
1 tablespoon malt vinegar	1 tablespoon malt vinegar
275 g/10 oz cod fillets, cut into pieces	10 oz cod or similar white fish fillets, cut into pieces
100 g/4 oz peeled prawns	⅔ cup shelled shrimp
salt and freshly ground pepper	salt and freshly ground pepper

Cook the noodles in boiling salted water for about 6 minutes or until tender. Drain, rinse and drain again.

Heat the oil in the wok. Add the spring onions (scallions), ginger, garlic and celery and stir-fry for 5 minutes. Add the chicken stock, soy sauce, honey and vinegar and bring to the boil, stirring. Add the cooked noodles and stir well. Gently stir in the cod and simmer until the fish will flake easily when tested with a fork.

Stir in the prawns (shrimp) and salt and pepper to taste, about 2 minutes before serving.
Serves 4

Fish Curry

METRIC/IMPERIAL	AMERICAN
1-2 tablespoons oil	1-2 tablespoons oil
1 small onion, finely chopped	1 small onion, finely chopped
1 clove garlic, finely chopped	1 clove garlic, finely chopped
1 small eating apple, peeled, cored and chopped	1 small apple, peeled, cored and chopped
25 g/1 oz flour	¼ cup flour
1 tablespoon curry powder	1 tablespoon curry powder
150 ml/¼ pint cider	⅔ cup apple cider
1 chicken stock cube, dissolved in 300 ml/ ½ pint boiling water	1 chicken bouillon cube, dissolved in 1¼ cups boiling water
2 whole cloves	2 whole cloves
4 tomatoes, skinned and quartered	4 tomatoes, peeled and quartered
25 g/1 oz sultanas	2½ tablespoons golden raisins
2 teaspoons tomato purée	2 teaspoons tomato paste
2 tablespoons mango chutney	2 tablespoons mango chutney
1 tablespoon peeled and grated root ginger	1 tablespoon peeled and grated ginger root
750 g/1½ lb haddock, cod or plaice, skinned and cut into bite-size pieces	1½ lb haddock, cod or flounder, cut into bite-size pieces

Heat the oil in the wok. Add the onion, garlic and apple and stir-fry for 5 minutes or until browned. Add the flour and curry powder and cook for a few minutes, stirring. Gradually stir in the cider and stock (bouillon). Add the cloves, tomatoes, sultanas (golden raisins), tomato purée (paste), chutney and ginger. Bring to the boil and simmer for 10 minutes.

Add the fish and simmer gently for about 15 minutes or until the fish will flake easily when tested with a fork.

Serves 4

Prawn (Shrimp) and Almond Stir-Fry

METRIC/IMPERIAL	AMERICAN
about 2 tablespoons oil	about 2 tablespoons oil
1 large onion, chopped	1 large onion, chopped
2 sticks celery, chopped	2 stalks celery, chopped
1 green pepper, cored, seeded and chopped	1 green pepper, seeded and chopped
100 g/4 oz bamboo shoots, chopped	1 cup chopped bamboo shoots
50 g/2 oz water chestnuts, chopped	½ cup chopped water chestnuts
50 g/2 oz mushrooms, chopped	½ cup chopped mushrooms
225 g/8 oz peeled prawns	½ lb shelled shrimp
1 tablespoon soy sauce	1 tablespoon soy sauce
salt and freshly ground pepper	salt and freshly ground pepper
1½ tablespoons cornflour, dissolved in 120 ml/4 fl oz water	1½ tablespoons cornstarch, dissolved in ½ cup water
50 g/2 oz almonds, toasted	½ cup toasted almonds

Heat the oil in the wok. Add the onion and stir-fry for 3 minutes. Add the celery and green pepper and stir-fry for 2 minutes. Stir in the bamboo shoots, water chestnuts, mushrooms, prawns (shrimp), soy sauce and salt and pepper to taste. Cover with the lid and cook for 2 minutes, stirring occasionally.

Stir in the cornflour (cornstarch) mixture and cook until thickened. Stir in the almonds and serve.

Serves 4

Oriental Seafood and Mushrooms

METRIC/IMPERIAL	AMERICAN
2 tablespoons pure sesame oil	2 tablespoons pure sesame oil
3 tablespoons soy sauce	3 tablespoons soy sauce
1 teaspoon ground ginger	1 teaspoon ground ginger
pinch of cayenne or black pepper	pinch of cayenne or black pepper
1 clove garlic, finely chopped	1 clove garlic, finely chopped
1 spring onion, finely chopped	1 scallion, finely chopped
225 g/8 oz mushrooms, sliced	2 cups sliced mushrooms
2 sticks celery, diced	2 stalks celery, diced
225 g/8 oz peeled prawns, or canned and drained prawns	½ lb shelled shrimp, or canned and drained shrimp

Heat the sesame oil with the soy sauce, ginger, pepper, garlic and spring onion (scallion) in the wok. When the garlic is lightly browned, add the mushrooms and celery. Stir-fry for about 3 minutes or until completely coated with the sesame and spice mixture.

Stir in the prawns (shrimp) and cook for a further minute or until heated through. Serve with boiled white or brown rice.
Serves 4

Kedgeree

METRIC/IMPERIAL	AMERICAN
2 tablespoons oil	2 tablespoons oil
15 g/½ oz butter	1 tablespoon butter
1 onion, chopped	1 onion, chopped
450 g/1 lb cooked smoked haddock, cut into bite-size pieces	1 lb cooked smoked haddock (finnan haddie), cut into bite-size pieces
175 g/6 oz long-grain rice, cooked	1 cup long-grain rice, cooked
2 teaspoons made mustard	2 teaspoons prepared English mustard
2 hard-boiled eggs, roughly chopped	2 hard-cooked eggs, roughly chopped
salt and freshly ground pepper	salt and freshly ground pepper
1 tablespoon chopped parsley to garnish	1 tablespoon chopped parsley for garnish

Heat the oil and butter in the wok. Add the onion and fry for 5 minutes or until transparent. Add the fish, rice and mustard and toss in the oil and butter to coat and heat through.

Mix in the eggs and salt and pepper to taste. Cover with the lid and cook for 1 minute. Garnish with parsley.
Serves 4

Spiced Fish Parcels

METRIC/IMPERIAL	AMERICAN
25 g/1 oz butter	2 tablespoons butter
2 onions, chopped	2 onions, chopped
350 g/12 oz white fish fillets, skinned and cut into strips	¾ lb white fish fillets, cut into strips
1 teaspoon peeled and grated root ginger	1 teaspoon peeled and grated ginger root
¼ teaspoon chilli seasoning	¼ teaspoon chili seasoning
½ teaspoon sugar	½ teaspoon sugar
1 teaspoon wine vinegar	1 teaspoon wine vinegar
1 tablespoon flour	1 tablespoon flour
salt and freshly ground pepper	salt and freshly ground pepper
8 large cabbage leaves, boiled for 5 minutes and drained	8 large cabbage leaves, boiled for 5 minutes and drained

Melt the butter in the wok. Add the onions and fry for 5 minutes. Tip into a mixing bowl and add the fish, grated ginger, chilli seasoning, sugar, vinegar, flour and salt and pepper to taste. Mix well together.

Flatten and smooth out the cabbage leaves. Divide the fish mixture between the leaves. Roll up to make parcels, securing with wooden cocktail sticks (toothpicks) or string.

Wipe out or wash the wok. Place the fish parcels on a heatproof plate on a steaming rack over simmering water in the wok. Cover with the lid and steam for about 20 minutes.
Serves 4

Kedgeree
(Photograph: Colman's Mustard)

Tuna or Salmon Kedgeree

METRIC/IMPERIAL	AMERICAN
1 tablespoon oil	1 tablespoon oil
50 g/2 oz butter	¼ cup butter
1 onion, chopped	1 onion, chopped
½ cucumber, peeled and diced	½ cucumber, peeled and diced
1 tablespoon lemon juice	1 tablespoon lemon juice
225 g/8 oz long-grain rice, cooked	1¼ cups long-grain rice, cooked
1 × 225 g/8 oz can tuna or salmon, drained and flaked	1 can (8 oz) tuna or salmon, drained and flaked
4 hard-boiled eggs, chopped	4 hard-cooked eggs, chopped
2 tablespoons sweetcorn kernels	2 tablespoons whole kernel corn
1 tablespoon chopped parsley	1 tablespoon chopped parsley
salt and freshly ground pepper	salt and freshly ground pepper

Heat the oil and butter in the wok. Add the onion and fry for 3 minutes. Add the cucumber and lemon juice and stir-fry for 3 minutes. Stir in the rice, tuna or salmon, chopped eggs, corn, parsley and salt and pepper to taste. Heat through for 5 to 8 minutes.
Serves 4

Fish Fillets and Savoury Rice

METRIC/IMPERIAL	AMERICAN
40 g/1½ oz butter	3 tablespoons butter
1 tablespoon oil	1 tablespoon oil
3 rashers streaky bacon, rinds removed and chopped	3 slices bacon, chopped
50 g/2 oz halved almonds	½ cup halved almonds
4 large plaice fillets	4 large flounder fillets
flour	flour
225 g/8 oz long-grain rice, cooked	1¼ cups long-grain rice, cooked
25 g/1 oz capers, chopped	¼ cup chopped capers
salt and freshly ground pepper	salt and freshly ground pepper
lemon wedges to garnish	lemon wedges for garnish

Heat the butter and oil in the wok. Add the bacon and almonds and stir-fry until browned. Drain and remove from the wok.

Dust the fish lightly with flour. Add to the wok and fry gently for about 5 minutes or until the fish will flake easily when tested with a fork. Carefully remove and arrange on a heated serving dish.

Add the cooked rice to the wok and heat through. Stir in the bacon, almonds, capers and salt and pepper to taste. Arrange at either end of the serving dish or in a separate dish. Garnish the fish with lemon wedges and serve.
Serves 4

Sweet and Sour Prawns (Shrimp)

METRIC/IMPERIAL	AMERICAN
225 g/8 oz peeled prawns	½ lb shelled shrimp
1 tablespoon dry sherry	1 tablespoon dry sherry
salt and freshly ground pepper	salt and freshly ground pepper
2 tablespoons oil	2 tablespoons oil
2 onions, sliced	2 onions, sliced
1 green pepper, cored, seeded and sliced	1 green pepper, seeded and sliced
150 ml/¼ pint chicken stock	⅔ cup chicken stock or broth
1 × 225 g/8 oz can pineapple pieces	1 can (8 oz) pineapple chunks
1 tablespoon cornflour	1 tablespoon cornstarch
1 tablespoon soy sauce	1 tablespoon soy sauce
about 75 g/3 oz sugar	about 6 tablespoons sugar

Sprinkle the prawns (shrimp) with the sherry and salt and pepper to taste. Leave to marinate for at least 1 hour.

Heat the oil in the wok. Add the onions and green pepper and stir-fry for 5 minutes. Add the chicken stock and pineapple. Cover with the lid and cook for 5 minutes. Blend the cornflour (cornstarch), soy sauce and sugar together and add to the wok. Stir until the mixture thickens.

Add the prawns (shrimp) and cook for 30 seconds. Cover with the lid, remove from the heat and leave for 2 minutes before serving.
Serves 4

Thailand-Style Fried Fish

METRIC/IMPERIAL	AMERICAN
6 dab fillets	6 small flounder fillets
flour	flour
4 tablespoons oil	¼ cup oil
450 g/1 lb bean sprouts	1 lb bean sprouts
100 g/4 oz button mushrooms, quartered	1 cup quartered mushrooms
15 g/½ oz lettuce, finely shredded	½ cup finely shredded lettuce
100 g/4 oz peeled prawns	⅔ cup shelled shrimp
1 tablespoon soy sauce	1 tablespoon soy sauce
lemon wedges	lemon wedges
Marinade:	**Marinade:**
1 tablespoon oil	1 tablespoon oil
1 tablespoon lemon juice	1 tablespoon lemon juice
salt and freshly ground pepper	salt and freshly ground pepper

Cut the fish fillets into 1 cm/½ inch wide strips and marinate in the oil, lemon juice and salt and pepper to taste for 30 minutes.

Drain the fish strips. Season flour with salt and pepper and lightly coat the fish strips. Heat 2 tablespoons of the oil in the wok. Add the fish and stir-fry for about 5 minutes. Remove and keep warm.

Heat the remaining oil in the wok. Stir in the bean sprouts and mushrooms and stir-fry for 2 to 3 minutes. Add the lettuce and prawns (shrimp), then stir in the soy sauce and heat through.

Gently fold in the fried fish, add more seasoning if necessary and serve hot. Serve with lemon wedges.
Serves 4

Fish Mediterranean

METRIC/IMPERIAL	AMERICAN
2 tablespoons oil	2 tablespoons oil
1 onion, chopped	1 onion, chopped
1 clove garlic, crushed	1 clove garlic, crushed
2 red or green peppers, cored, seeded and chopped	2 red or green peppers, seeded and chopped
1 × 57 g/2 oz can anchovy fillets, drained and chopped	1 can (2 oz) anchovy fillets, drained and chopped
1 × 425 g/15 oz can tomatoes, drained and chopped	1 can (16 oz) tomatoes, drained and chopped
½ teaspoon dried tarragon	½ teaspoon dried tarragon
450 g/1 lb cod or similar white fish fillet, skinned and cut into bite-size pieces	1 lb cod or similar white fish fillet, cut into bite-size pieces
freshly ground pepper	freshly ground pepper

Heat the oil in the wok. Add the onion, garlic, red or green peppers and anchovies and stir-fry for 5 to 8 minutes or until the onion and peppers are soft. Add the tomatoes, tarragon, fish and pepper to taste. Cook for about 10 minutes or until the fish will flake easily when tested with a fork.
Serves 4 to 5

Beef Dishes

Quick-Fried Beef with Peppers

METRIC/IMPERIAL	AMERICAN
350 g/12 oz steak, thinly sliced	¾ lb steak, thinly sliced
4 tablespoons oil	¼ cup oil
1 tablespoon cornflour	1 tablespoon cornstarch
½ teaspoon salt	½ teaspoon salt
1 jar Canton black bean stir-fry sauce	1 jar Canton black bean stir-fry sauce
2 medium green peppers, cored, seeded and roughly chopped	2 medium-size green peppers, seeded and roughly chopped

Toss the beef in a little of the oil, then dust with the cornflour (cornstarch) and sprinkle with the salt.

Heat the remaining oil in the wok. Add the beef and stir-fry for 1 to 2 minutes. Add the black bean sauce and cook, stirring, for 1 minute. Add the green peppers, toss with the beef and serve immediately.
Serves 3 to 4

For a complete Chinese meal, serve with soup, rice, Triple Layer Omelette (page 52), Hot Tossed Salad (page 62) and fruit, for 6 people.

Clockwise from front: Quick Fried Beef with Peppers; Hot Tossed Salad (page 62); Triple Layer Omelette (page 52), served with soup, rice and fruit
(Photograph: J A Sharwood Co Ltd)

Fried Beef and Pork Meat Balls

METRIC/IMPERIAL	AMERICAN
175 g/6 oz lean beef	6 oz lean beef
175 g/6 oz lean pork	6 oz lean pork
100 g/4 oz water chestnuts, roughly chopped	1 cup roughly chopped water chestnuts
salt and freshly ground pepper	salt and freshly ground pepper
2 eggs, separated	2 eggs, separated
2 tablespoons cornflour	2 tablespoons cornstarch
about 6 tablespoons oil	about 6 tablespoons oil
1 clove garlic, cut into thin strips	1 clove garlic, cut into thin strips
2.5 cm/1 inch piece root ginger, peeled and cut into thin strips	1 inch piece ginger root, peeled and cut into thin strips
2 tablespoons soy sauce	2 tablespoons soy sauce
3 tablespoons dry sherry	3 tablespoons dry sherry

Mince (grind) the beef, pork and water chestnuts together finely. Add salt and pepper to taste and bind with one beaten egg yolk. Roll into walnut-size balls. Mix the remaining whole egg with the egg white. Dip the meat balls into this and then into the cornflour (cornstarch). Repeat this coating process.

Heat the oil in the wok. Add the meat balls and stir-fry on all sides over high heat, then reduce the heat and continue cooking until tender. Add the garlic and ginger and stir-fry for 2 to 3 minutes longer. Sprinkle the meat balls with the soy sauce, sherry and pepper to taste. Serve with rice.
Serves 4

Beef Chow Mein

METRIC/IMPERIAL	AMERICAN
225-350 g/8-12 oz Chinese noodles	½-¾ lb Chinese noodles
225 g/8 oz braising steak, cut into thin strips	½ lb beef flank steak, cut into thin strips
4 tablespoons oil	¼ cup oil
3 tablespoons cornflour	3 tablespoons cornstarch
2 medium onions, thinly sliced	2 medium-size onions, thinly sliced
100 g/4 oz mushrooms	¼ lb mushrooms
1 red pepper, cored, seeded and sliced	1 red pepper, seeded and sliced
1 green pepper, cored, seeded and sliced	1 green pepper, seeded and sliced
2 tablespoons light soy sauce	2 tablespoons light soy sauce
2 tablespoons good quality oyster sauce	2 tablespoons good quality oyster sauce
2 tablespoons dry sherry	2 tablespoons dry sherry
100 g/4 oz cooked prawns with shells	¼ lb cooked shrimp with shells
3 spring onions, chopped	3 scallions, chopped

Cook the noodles in boiling salted water for 5 to 6 minutes. Drain and rinse. Toss the beef in a little of the oil, then dust with the cornflour (cornstarch).

Heat the remaining oil in the wok. Add the beef and stir-fry for 2 minutes. Push to one side. Add the onions, mushrooms and red and green peppers and stir-fry for 3 minutes. Return the beef with the soy sauce, oyster sauce, sherry, prawns (shrimp) and spring onions (scallions). Mix well, then add the noodles. Heat thoroughly.
Serves 3 to 4

For a complete Chinese meal, serve with Steamed Whole Fish (page 7), Braised Knuckle (Hock) of Pork (page 33), Lettuce in Oyster Sauce (page 56) and lychees, for 6 people.
Illustrated on page 6

Sweet and Sour Meat Balls

METRIC/IMPERIAL	AMERICAN
450 g/1 lb lean minced beef	1 lb lean ground beef
1 onion, finely chopped	1 onion, finely chopped
1 egg	1 egg
2 tablespoons soy sauce	2 tablespoons soy sauce
salt and freshly ground pepper	salt and freshly ground pepper
2 tablespoons oil	2 tablespoons oil
3 tablespoons brown sugar	3 tablespoons brown sugar
3 tablespoons cider vinegar	3 tablespoons cider vinegar
1 × 225 g/8 oz can pineapple pieces, drained	1 can (8 oz) pineapple chunks, drained
1 green pepper, cored, seeded and sliced	1 green pepper, seeded and sliced
2 tomatoes, skinned and roughly chopped	2 tomatoes, skinned and roughly chopped
2 tablespoons cornflour, dissolved in 120 ml/4 fl oz water	2 tablespoons cornstarch, dissolved in ½ cup water

Mix the beef, onion, egg, soy sauce and salt and pepper to taste together. Shape into very small meat balls. Heat the oil in the wok. Add the meat balls and fry for 10 to 15 minutes, depending on size, until browned on all sides and cooked through. Transfer to a heated serving dish and keep hot.

Wipe out the wok with kitchen paper towels. Add the sugar and vinegar to the wok and heat until the sugar has dissolved. Add the pineapple, green pepper and tomatoes and simmer for 3 minutes. Stir in the cornflour (cornstarch) mixture and stir for about 2 minutes or until thickened. Pour this sauce over the meat balls and serve.
Serves 4

Bolognese Sauce

METRIC/IMPERIAL	AMERICAN
50 g/2 oz butter	¼ cup butter
2 rashers bacon, rinds removed and chopped	2 slices bacon, chopped
1 onion, finely chopped	1 onion, finely chopped
2 carrots, finely chopped	2 carrots, finely chopped
2 sticks celery, finely chopped	2 stalks celery, finely chopped
450 g/1 lb minced beef	1 lb ground beef
300 ml/½ pint stock	1¼ cups stock or broth
150 ml/¼ pint white wine	⅔ cup white wine
1 × 225 g/8 oz can tomatoes, chopped	1 can (8 oz) tomatoes, chopped
1 tablespoon tomato purée	1 tablespoon tomato paste
1 teaspoon salt	1 teaspoon salt
freshly ground pepper	freshly ground pepper
grated nutmeg	grated nutmeg
100 g/4 oz mushrooms, sliced	1 cup sliced mushrooms
4 tablespoons double cream (optional)	¼ cup heavy cream (optional)

Heat the butter in the wok. Add the bacon and fry for 2 minutes. Add the onion, carrots and celery and stir-fry for 5 minutes. Add the beef and stir-fry for about 10 minutes or until browned and crumbly. Stir in the stock and wine. Simmer until the sauce thickens, stirring. Add the undrained tomatoes, tomato purée (paste), salt and pepper and nutmeg to taste. Cover with the lid and cook for 15 minutes. Add the mushrooms and cook for a further 5 minutes. If using, stir in the cream just before serving. Serve over buttered spaghetti seasoned with grated nutmeg.
Serves 4 to 6

Beef with Oyster Sauce

METRIC/IMPERIAL	AMERICAN
450 g/1 lb good quality steak, cut into thin strips	1 lb good quality steak, cut into thin strips
1 tablespoon cornflour	1 tablespoon cornstarch
4 tablespoons corn oil	¼ cup corn oil
1 onion, quartered and separated	1 onion, quartered and separated
1 green pepper, cored, seeded and sliced	1 green pepper, seeded and sliced
150 ml/¼ pint oyster sauce	⅔ cup oyster sauce
1 small can water chestnuts, drained and sliced	1 small can water chestnuts, drained and sliced

Toss the meat lightly in the cornflour (cornstarch).

Heat 2 tablespoons of the oil in the wok and fry the onion and green pepper for 2 minutes, then push to one side of the wok. Add the remaining oil and stir-fry the meat over a high heat for 2 minutes. Stir in the oyster sauce and water chestnuts and stir together with the onion and green pepper. Heat through thoroughly and serve on a warm plate.
Serves 4
Illustrated on page 35

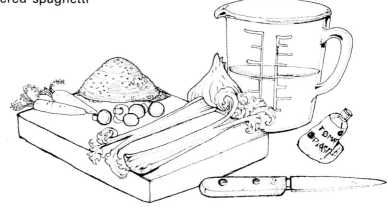

Meat Ball Curry

METRIC/IMPERIAL	AMERICAN
450 g/1 lb minced beef	1 lb ground beef
2 large onions, chopped	2 large onions, chopped
4 cloves garlic, chopped	4 cloves garlic, chopped
2 teaspoons turmeric	2 teaspoons turmeric
2 teaspoons chilli powder	2 teaspoons chili powder
2 teaspoons ground coriander	2 teaspoons ground coriander
1½ teaspoons ground cumin	1½ teaspoons ground cumin
1 teaspoon ground ginger	1 teaspoon ground ginger
2 teaspoons salt	2 teaspoons salt
1 egg, beaten	1 egg, beaten
oil for deep-frying	oil for deep-frying
100 g/4 oz clarified butter or 4 tablespoons oil	½ cup clarified butter or ¼ cup oil
200 ml/⅓ pint water	1 cup water
mint leaves to garnish	mint leaves for garnish

Put the beef in a bowl and add half the onions, garlic, spices and salt. Stir well, then bind the mixture together with the beaten egg.

Form the mixture into 12 small balls. Heat enough oil in the wok for deep-frying. Add the meat balls a few at a time and deep-fry for 5 minutes. Remove from the pan with a slotted spoon, drain on kitchen paper towels and set aside. Pour the oil from the wok and wipe it out.

Heat the butter or oil in the wok, add the remaining onions and garlic and fry until soft. Add the remaining spices and salt and stir-fry for a further 3 minutes. Add the meat balls and turn gently to coat with the spices, then add the water and bring to the boil. Lower the heat and simmer gently for 30 minutes.

Serve hot, garnished with mint leaves.
Serves 4

Chilli Con Carne

METRIC/IMPERIAL	AMERICAN
1 tablespoon oil	1 tablespoon oil
1 large onion, chopped	1 large onion, chopped
450-650 g/1-1¼ lb lean minced beef	1-1¼ lb lean ground beef
1 clove garlic, crushed	1 clove garlic, crushed
100 g/4 oz mushrooms, sliced (optional)	1 cup sliced mushrooms (optional)
1 green pepper, cored, seeded and chopped	1 green pepper, seeded and chopped
1 × 425 g/15 oz can tomatoes	1 can (16 oz) tomatoes
1-2 teaspoons chilli powder, according to taste	1-2 teaspoons chili powder, according to taste
salt and freshly ground pepper	salt and freshly ground pepper
1 tablespoon wine vinegar	1 tablespoon wine vinegar
1 teaspoon sugar	1 teaspoon sugar
2 tablespoons tomato purée	2 tablespoons tomato paste
1 × 425 g/15 oz can red kidney beans, drained	1 can (16 oz) red kidney beans, drained

Heat the oil in the wok. Add the onion and fry for 2 minutes. Add the beef, garlic, mushrooms, if used, and green pepper and stir-fry for about 5 minutes or until the meat changes colour. Add the undrained tomatoes, chilli powder and salt and pepper to taste. Cover with the lid and simmer for 10 minutes. Stir in the vinegar, sugar, tomato purée (paste) and beans and cook, uncovered, for a further 10 minutes.
Serves 4

Clockwise from front: Meat Ball Curry, Calcutta Beef Curry (page 20): Spiced Aubergines (Eggplants) and Tomatoes (page 55)

Steak and Mushrooms

METRIC/IMPERIAL	AMERICAN
75 g/3 oz butter	6 tablespoons butter
1 large onion, chopped	1 large onion, chopped
2 cloves garlic, crushed	2 cloves garlic, crushed
175 g/6 oz mushrooms, sliced	1½ cups sliced mushrooms
4 teaspoons French mustard	4 teaspoons Dijon-style mustard
4 steaks	4 steaks
salt and freshly ground pepper	salt and freshly ground pepper
1 tablespoon soy sauce	1 tablespoon soy sauce
1 tablespoon tomato purée	1 tablespoon tomato paste
watercress to garnish	watercress for garnish

Heat the butter in the wok. Add the onion and garlic and stir-fry for 3 minutes. Add the mushrooms and stir-fry for a further 3 minutes. Spread the mustard on to both sides of the steaks and sprinkle with salt and pepper. Push the onions and mushrooms to one side and fry the steaks in the wok on both sides until cooked to personal taste. Remove the steaks to a heated serving dish.

Stir the soy sauce and tomato purée (paste) into the onion and mushroom mixture. Cook for 1 minute, then spoon over the steaks. Garnish with watercress.
Serves 4

Beef Stroganoff

METRIC/IMPERIAL	AMERICAN
50 g/2 oz butter	¼ cup butter
1 onion, finely chopped	1 onion, finely chopped
100 g/4 oz mushrooms, sliced	1 cup sliced mushrooms
450-650 g/1-1¼ lb good quality steak, cut into thin strips	1-1¼ lb good quality steak, cut into thin strips
2 teaspoons flour	2 teaspoons flour
150 ml/¼ pint soured cream	⅔ cup sour cream
2 teaspoons French mustard	2 teaspoons Dijon-style mustard
salt and freshly ground pepper	salt and freshly ground pepper

Heat the butter in the wok. Add the onion and fry for 3 minutes. Add the mushrooms and stir-fry for 3 minutes. Push to one side. Add the steak to the wok and stir-fry for about 5 minutes or until sealed on all sides and just cooked. Sprinkle over the flour and mix in. Add the soured cream, mustard and salt and pepper to taste. Mix all the ingredients together gently. Serve with rice or noodles and a salad.
Serves 4

Calcutta Beef Curry

METRIC/IMPERIAL	AMERICAN
1½ teaspoons ground coriander	1½ teaspoons ground coriander
1 teaspoon turmeric	1 teaspoon turmeric
1 teaspoon ground cumin	1 teaspoon ground cumin
1½ teaspoons salt	1½ teaspoons salt
1 teaspoon pepper	1 teaspoon pepper
1 tablespoon milk	1 tablespoon milk
50 g/2 oz clarified butter or 2 tablespoons oil	¼ cup clarified butter or oil
1 small onion, sliced	1 small onion, sliced
1 clove garlic, sliced	1 clove garlic, sliced
450 g/1 lb good quality steak, cut into 2.5 cm/1 inch cubes	1 lb good quality steak, cut into 1 inch cubes
120 ml/4 fl oz water	½ cup water
chopped mint or coriander leaves to garnish	chopped mint or coriander leaves for garnish

Mix the spices and seasonings to a paste with the milk. Heat the butter or oil in the wok, add the onion and garlic and fry until soft. Stir in the paste and fry for a further 1 minute. Push to one side. Add the steak and stir-fry until browned on all sides. Stir in the water and bring to the boil. Simmer for 3 minutes. Sprinkle with mint or coriander and serve hot.
Serves 4
Illustrated on page 19

Stir-Fried Beef with Asparagus

METRIC/IMPERIAL	AMERICAN
225 g/8 oz lean steak, thinly sliced	½ lb lean steak, thinly sliced
2 tablespoons soy sauce	2 tablespoons soy sauce
2 tablespoons wine	2 tablespoons wine
salt	salt
3 tablespoons oil	3 tablespoons oil
1 onion, thinly sliced	1 onion, thinly sliced
350 g/12 oz asparagus, sliced diagonally	¾ lb asparagus, sliced diagonally
5 tablespoons water	5 tablespoons water
2 sticks celery, sliced diagonally	2 stalks celery, sliced diagonally
1 tablespoon cornflour, dissolved in 2 tablespoons water	1 tablespoon cornstarch, dissolved in 2 tablespoons water

Marinate the beef in the soy sauce, wine and salt to taste. Leave for 30 minutes. Heat the oil in the wok. Add the beef and onion and stir-fry for about 5 minutes. Remove and keep warm. Add the asparagus to the wok with the water. Stir, cover with the lid and cook for 3 minutes, stirring occasionally. Add the celery, cover and cook for a further 3 to 6 minutes or until the asparagus is lightly cooked. Return the beef and onion. Stir in the cornflour (cornstarch) mixture and heat through for 2 to 3 minutes.
Serves 3

Italian Beef

METRIC/IMPERIAL	AMERICAN
40 g/1½ oz butter	3 tablespoons butter
1 onion, chopped	1 onion, chopped
1 green pepper, cored, seeded and thinly sliced	1 green pepper, seeded and thinly sliced
100 g/4 oz mushrooms, sliced	1 cup sliced mushrooms
350 g/12 oz rump steak, cut into strips	¾ lb top round steak, cut into strips
25 g/1 oz flour	¼ cup flour
300 ml/½ pint beef stock	1¼ cups beef stock or broth
2 tablespoons tomato purée	2 tablespoons tomato paste
salt and freshly ground pepper	salt and freshly ground pepper

Heat the butter in the wok. Add the onion and green pepper and stir-fry for 5 minutes. Add the mushrooms and stir-fry for a further 3 minutes. Push to one side. Add the beef and stir-fry for 3 to 5 minutes or until browned. Sprinkle on the flour and stir into all the ingredients. Add the stock, tomato purée (paste) and salt and pepper to taste, stir well and cook for about 5 minutes longer.
Serves 4

Beef Chop Suey

METRIC/IMPERIAL	AMERICAN
450 g/1 lb braising steak, trimmed and cut into thin strips	1 lb flank steak, trimmed and cut into thin strips
1 tablespoon sherry	1 tablespoon sherry
3 tablespoons soy sauce	3 tablespoons soy sauce
2 tablespoons corn oil	2 tablespoons corn oil
1 onion, sliced	1 onion, sliced
2 sticks celery, chopped	2 stalks celery, chopped
2 carrots, cut into thin strips	2 carrots, cut into thin strips
100 g/4 oz mushrooms, sliced	1 cup sliced mushrooms
1 tablespoon demerara sugar	1 tablespoon raw brown sugar
1 beef stock cube, dissolved in 150 ml/¼ pint boiling water	1 beef bouillon cube, dissolved in ⅔ cup boiling water
100-175 g/4-6 oz bean sprouts	2-3 cups bean sprouts

Marinate the steak in the sherry and soy sauce for 10 minutes. Heat the oil in the wok. Add the meat and stir-fry for 3 to 4 minutes. Remove and keep warm. Add the onion, celery, carrots and mushrooms to the wok and stir-fry for 3 to 4 minutes. Stir in the sugar, stock (bouillon) and bean sprouts. Return the meat to the wok and cook for a further 2 minutes. Serve with boiled or fried rice and tomato wedges.
Serves 4

Lamb Dishes

Marinated Stir-Fried Lamb

METRIC/IMPERIAL	AMERICAN
750 g/1½ lb lamb shoulder meat, cut into 1 cm/½ inch cubes	1½ lb lamb shoulder meat, cut into ½ inch cubes
4 teaspoons oil	4 teaspoons oil
150 ml/¼ pint chicken stock	⅔ cup chicken stock or broth
2 sticks celery, sliced diagonally	2 stalks celery, sliced diagonally
100 g/4 oz cabbage, shredded	1 cup shredded cabbage
2 tablespoons sliced stem ginger, or ¼ teaspoon ground ginger	2 tablespoons sliced preserved ginger, or ¼ teaspoon ground ginger
Marinade:	**Marinade:**
3 tablespoons soy sauce	3 tablespoons soy sauce
2 tablespoons vinegar	2 tablespoons vinegar
2 tablespoons brown sugar	2 tablespoons brown sugar
1 clove garlic, crushed	1 clove garlic, crushed

Prepare the marinade by mixing together all the ingredients. Soak the lamb in the marinade for 2 hours or, preferably, overnight.

Drain the lamb from the marinade. Heat 3 teaspoons of the oil in the wok. Add the lamb and stir-fry for 5 to 8 minutes. Add the stock and cook for a further 10 minutes (the liquid should reduce). Remove the lamb and keep warm. Heat the remaining oil in the wok. Add the celery, cabbage and ginger and stir-fry for 2 to 3 minutes. Stir the lamb into the vegetables and heat through.
Serves 4

Marinated Stir-Fried Lamb
(Photograph: New Zealand Lamb Information Bureau)

Lamb with Broccoli

METRIC/IMPERIAL	AMERICAN
2 tablespoons oil	2 tablespoons oil
2 sticks celery, sliced diagonally into 1 cm/½ inch pieces	2 stalks celery, sliced diagonally into ½ inch pieces
1 medium onion, thinly sliced	1 medium-size onion, thinly sliced
100 g/4 oz broccoli, cut into small florets	¼ lb broccoli, cut into small flowerettes
4 tablespoons water	¼ cup water
450 g/1 lb lamb from the shoulder, cut into thin strips	1 lb lamb from the shoulder, cut into thin strips
1 tablespoon soy sauce	1 tablespoon soy sauce
1 tablespoon tomato purée	1 tablespoon tomato paste
150 ml/¼ pint chicken stock	⅔ cup chicken stock or broth
salt and freshly ground pepper	salt and freshly ground pepper
1 tablespoon cornflour dissolved in 2 tablespoons water	1 tablespoon cornstarch dissolved in 2 tablespoons water

Heat 1 tablespoon of the oil in the wok. Add the celery, onion and broccoli and stir-fry for about 3 minutes. Add the water, cover with the lid and steam for 5 to 8 minutes, stirring occasionally, until the broccoli is almost tender. Remove the vegetables from the wok and keep warm.

Heat the remaining oil in the wok. Add the lamb and stir-fry for 5 minutes or until browned. Add the soy sauce, tomato purée (paste), stock and salt and pepper to taste, and simmer for 15 minutes. Return the vegetables to the wok and heat through. Add the cornflour (cornstarch) mixture and stir to thicken the juices. Cook for a further 5 minutes.
Serves 4

Lamb Cooked in Red Wine

METRIC/IMPERIAL
50 g/2 oz butter
750 g/1½ lb lamb
   from the top of the
   leg, cubed
225 g/8 oz small
   onions or shallots
4 rashers streaky
   bacon, rinds
   removed and
   roughly chopped
1 clove garlic,
   crushed
2 sticks celery, sliced
100 g/4 oz button
   mushrooms
300 ml/½ pint red
   wine
1 bay leaf
salt and freshly
   ground pepper
25 g/1 oz flour

AMERICAN
¼ cup butter
1½ lb lamb from the
   top of the leg,
   cubed
½ lb small onions or
   shallots
4 slices bacon,
   roughly chopped
1 clove garlic,
   crushed
2 stalks celery, sliced
1 cup button
   mushrooms
1¼ cups red wine
1 bay leaf
salt and freshly
   ground pepper
¼ cup flour

Heat 25 g/1 oz (2 tablespoons) of the butter in the wok. Add the lamb and fry until browned on all sides, stirring occasionally. Push to one side. Add the onions and stir-fry for 3 minutes. Add the bacon, garlic and celery and stir-fry for a further 5 minutes. Stir the mushrooms, wine, bay leaf and salt and pepper to taste into the lamb mixture. Cover with the lid and simmer for about 40 minutes or until the lamb is tender. Remove the bay leaf.

Blend the remaining butter and flour together to make a paste. Stir pieces of this into the wok. Heat until thickened.
Serves 6

Curried Lamb with Yogurt

METRIC/IMPERIAL
1 tablespoon oil
1 large onion,
   chopped
750 g/1½ lb lamb
   from the shoulder,
   cubed
1 clove garlic,
   crushed
2 small chillies,
   chopped
1 tablespoon peeled
   and finely chopped
   root ginger, or
   1 teaspoon ground
   ginger
2 tomatoes, skinned
   and chopped
150 ml/¼ pint plain
   yogurt
150 ml/¼ pint water
salt and freshly
   ground pepper

AMERICAN
1 tablespoon oil
1 large onion,
   chopped
1½ lb lamb from the
   shoulder, cubed
1 clove garlic,
   crushed
2 small chili peppers,
   chopped
1 tablespoon peeled
   and finely chopped
   ginger root, or
   1 teaspoon ground
   ginger
2 tomatoes, peeled
   and chopped
⅔ cup plain yogurt
⅔ cup water
salt and freshly
   ground pepper

Heat the oil in the wok. Add the onion, lamb and garlic and stir-fry for 5 minutes or until the meat is browned. Add the chillies, ginger, tomatoes, yogurt, water and salt and pepper to taste. Cover with the lid and simmer for about 45 minutes, stirring occasionally, until the lamb is almost cooked. Remove the lid and simmer for a further 10 to 15 minutes or until the liquid has reduced a little.
Serves 4

Meat Balls with Barbecue Sauce

METRIC/IMPERIAL	AMERICAN
450 g/1 lb minced lamb	1 lb ground lamb
1 large onion, grated	1 large onion, grated
salt and freshly ground pepper	salt and freshly ground pepper
flour	flour
beaten egg and fresh breadcrumbs to coat	beaten egg and soft bread crumbs to coat
oil for deep frying	oil for deep frying
Barbecue sauce:	**Barbecue sauce:**
2 tablespoons tomato ketchup	2 tablespoons tomato ketchup
1 tablespoon Worcestershire sauce	1 tablespoon Worcestershire sauce
1 tablespoon fruity sauce	1 tablespoon chop sauce
2 teaspoons honey	2 teaspoons honey
1 teaspoon French mustard	1 teaspoon Dijon-style mustard

Combine the lamb, onion and salt and pepper to taste. Divide into 20 meat balls. Season flour with salt and pepper and use to coat the meat balls, then coat in beaten egg and breadcrumbs. Heat about 7.5 cm/3 inches of oil in the wok to 190°C/375°F. Add the meat balls, a few at a time, and deep-fry for 8 to 10 minutes. Drain on kitchen paper towels and keep hot.

To make the barbecue sauce, combine all the ingredients, with salt and pepper to taste. Serve with the meat balls.
Serves 4 to 5

Lamb in Soured Cream

METRIC/IMPERIAL	AMERICAN
25 g/1 oz flour	¼ cup flour
½ teaspoon salt	½ teaspoon salt
¼ teaspoon pepper	¼ teaspoon pepper
½ teaspoon dried thyme	½ teaspoon dried thyme
8 noisettes of lamb	8 boned and rolled lamb rib chops
40 g/1½ oz butter	3 tablespoons butter
1 onion, thinly sliced	1 onion, thinly sliced
1 beef stock cube, dissolved in 4 tablespoons boiling water	1 beef bouillon cube, dissolved in ¼ cup boiling water
150 ml/¼ pint soured cream	⅔ cup sour cream
225 g/8 oz mushrooms, sliced	2 cups sliced mushrooms

Mix the flour, salt, pepper and thyme together. Coat the lamb with this mixture.

Heat the butter in the wok. Add the meat and fry until browned on both sides. Add the onion and fry for 5 minutes or until transparent. Pour the stock (bouillon) over the lamb. Cover with the lid and braise over a low heat for 40 minutes or until the lamb is tender. Check halfway through cooking there is enough liquid to prevent the lamb sticking. Add the soured cream and mushrooms and heat gently for 5 minutes. Serve with noodles or rice.
Serves 4

Lamb Steaks with Lemon

METRIC/IMPERIAL
450 g/1 lb lamb, thinly
  sliced from the leg
flour
salt and freshly
  ground pepper
1-2 tablespoons oil
4-6 tablespoons beef
  stock
½ lemon, cut into
  paper-thin slices
22 g/¾ oz butter
1 tablespoon lemon
  juice

AMERICAN
1 lb lamb, thinly
  sliced from the leg
flour
salt and freshly
  ground pepper
1-2 tablespoons oil
4-6 tablespoons beef
  stock or broth
½ lemon, cut into
  paper-thin slices
1½ tablespoons
  butter
1 tablespoon lemon
  juice

Pound the slices of lamb with a meat mallet or rolling pin. Season the flour with salt and pepper and use to coat the lamb. Heat the oil in the wok. Add the lamb and fry until browned on both sides. Stir in the stock and place a lemon slice on top of each lamb steak. Cover with the lid and simmer gently for 10 to 15 minutes. Remove the lamb and keep warm. Add the butter to the wok with the lemon juice and salt and pepper if required. Heat through and spoon over the lamb.

Garnish with fresh lemon slices.
Serves 4

Orange Braised Lamb

METRIC/IMPERIAL
2 large oranges
4 lamb leg bone
  steaks
salt and freshly
  ground pepper
about 1 tablespoon
  oil
6 spring onions,
  shredded
150 ml/¼ pint stock
25 g/1 oz brown sugar

AMERICAN
2 large oranges
4 lamb sirloin chops
salt and freshly
  ground pepper
about 1 tablespoon
  oil
6 scallions, shredded
⅔ cup stock or broth
2½ tablespoons
  brown sugar

Thinly pare the rind from the oranges with a potato peeler. Shred the rind finely, blanch in boiling water for 5 minutes and drain.

Sprinkle the lamb with salt and pepper. Heat the oil in the wok. Add the lamb and fry until browned on both sides. Remove from the wok. Add the onions to the wok and fry for 3 minutes. Place the lamb on top of the onions. Add the juice squeezed from the oranges, the stock, brown sugar, orange rind shreds and salt and pepper to taste. Cover with the lid and braise over a low heat for 40 minutes or until the lamb is tender.
Serves 4

Orange Braised Lamb
(Photograph: New Zealand Lamb Information
Bureau)

Piquant Liver Stir-Fry

METRIC/IMPERIAL	AMERICAN
1 tablespoon oil	1 tablespoon oil
25 g/1 oz butter	2 tablespoons butter
1 onion, chopped	1 onion, chopped
1 clove garlic, crushed	1 clove garlic, crushed
1 tablespoon peeled and grated root ginger	1 tablespoon peeled and grated ginger root
½ green pepper, cored, seeded and chopped	½ green pepper, seeded and chopped
3 tablespoons flour	3 tablespoons flour
salt and freshly ground pepper	salt and freshly ground pepper
350-450 g/12 oz-1 lb lamb's liver, cut into strips	¾-1 lb lamb liver, cut into strips
1 tablespoon dry sherry	1 tablespoon dry sherry

Heat the oil and butter in the wok. Add the onion, garlic, ginger and green pepper and stir-fry for 5 minutes. Push to one side. Season the flour with salt and pepper and use to coat the liver. Add the liver to the wok and stir-fry for about 5 minutes. Add the sherry and salt and pepper if required and stir all the ingredients together. Cook for a further 5 minutes or until the liver is just cooked. Serve with hot buttered noodles or mashed potatoes.
Serves 4

Ragoût of Liver

METRIC/IMPERIAL	AMERICAN
25 g/1 oz flour	¼ cup flour
salt and freshly ground pepper	salt and freshly ground pepper
450 g/1 lb lamb's liver, sliced	1 lb lamb liver, sliced
2 tablespoons oil	2 tablespoons oil
1 onion, sliced	1 onion, sliced
4 rashers bacon, rinds removed and chopped	4 slices bacon, chopped
450 ml/¾ pint stock	2 cups stock or broth
25 g/1 oz sultanas	2½ tablespoons golden raisins
1 apple, peeled, cored and grated	1 apple, peeled, cored and grated
1 teaspoon tomato purée	1 teaspoon tomato paste

Season the flour with salt and pepper and use to coat the liver. Heat the oil in the wok. Add the liver, onion and bacon and stir-fry until golden brown. Stir in the stock and bring to the boil. Add the sultanas (golden raisins), apple and tomato purée (paste). Lower the heat and simmer for 15 to 20 minutes.
Serves 4

Kidneys in White Wine Sauce

METRIC/IMPERIAL	AMERICAN
75 g/3 oz butter	6 tablespoons butter
12 lamb's kidneys, skinned, cored and thickly sliced	12 lamb kidneys, skinned, cored and thickly sliced
1 onion, finely chopped	1 onion, finely chopped
150 ml/¼ pint dry white wine	⅔ cup dry white wine
1 tablespoon lemon juice	1 tablespoon lemon juice
1½ tablespoons made French or English mustard	1½ tablespoons Dijon-style or prepared English mustard

Heat 50 g/2 oz (¼ cup) of the butter in the wok. Add the kidneys and fry for 5 minutes, stirring occasionally to cook on all sides. Do not overcook. The kidneys should stiffen and brown slightly without becoming hard and dry. Push to one side or remove and keep warm.

Add the onion to the wok and fry for 3 to 5 minutes or until soft and transparent. Add the wine and lemon juice, increase the heat and boil until the liquid has reduced to about two-thirds. Mix the mustard and remaining butter together. Stir the mustard butter into the wine mixture in spoonfuls. Return the kidneys to the sauce together with any juices which may have drained from them. Reheat without boiling. Serve the kidneys on boiled rice with the sauce poured over them, accompanied by a green salad.
Serves 4

Sweet and Sour Kidney Flowers

METRIC/IMPERIAL	AMERICAN
450 g/1 lb lamb's kidneys, skinned, cored and halved	1 lb lamb kidneys, skinned, cored and halved
1 tablespoon cornflour	1 tablespoon cornstarch
4 tablespoons oil	¼ cup oil
1 onion, thinly sliced	1 onion, thinly sliced
1 pepper, cored, seeded and thinly sliced	1 pepper, seeded and thinly sliced
2-3 slices pickled or peeled root ginger	2-3 sliced pickled ginger or peeled ginger root
1 jar Peking sweet and sour stir-fry sauce	1 jar Peking sweet and sour stir-fry sauce

Cut a criss-cross design two-thirds through each kidney half. Dust with the cornflour (cornstarch) and rub with a little of the oil. Heat the remaining oil in the wok. Add the onion and fry for 1 minute. Add the kidneys and fry over high heat for 1½ minutes, stirring occasionally to cook on all sides. Add the pepper and ginger and stir-fry for 1 minute. Pour in the sweet and sour sauce and toss all the ingredients together.
Serves 4

Curried Kidneys

METRIC/IMPERIAL	AMERICAN
50 g/2 oz butter	¼ cup butter
8 lamb's kidneys, skinned, cored and cut into pieces	8 lamb kidneys, skinned, cored and cut into pieces
1 onion, chopped	1 onion, chopped
2 parsnips, finely chopped	2 parsnips, finely chopped
about 2 tablespoons curry powder	about 2 tablespoons curry powder
2 apples, cored and chopped	2 apples, cored and chopped
50 g/2 oz sultanas	⅓ cup golden raisins
25 g/1 oz flour	¼ cup flour
300 ml/½ pint stock	1¼ cups stock or broth

Heat the butter in the wok. Add the kidneys and fry for 5 minutes, stirring occasionally to cook on all sides. Push to one side or remove and keep warm. Add the onion and parsnips and stir-fry for 3 minutes. Stir in the curry powder, apples, sultanas (golden raisins) and flour. Mix well before stirring in the stock and kidneys. Simmer for 10 minutes.
Serves 4

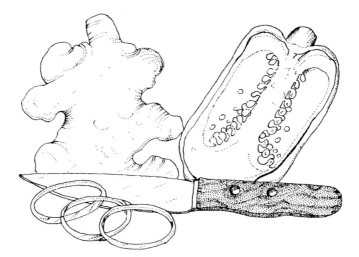

Pork Dishes

Pork and Pineapple Stir-Fry

METRIC/IMPERIAL	AMERICAN
2 tablespoons corn oil	2 tablespoons corn oil
450 g/1 lb pork fillet, cut into thin strips	1 lb pork tenderloin, cut into thin strips
2 tablespoons soy sauce	2 tablespoons soy sauce
1 tablespoon sherry	1 tablespoon sherry
2 teaspoons brown sugar	2 teaspoons brown sugar
3 small carrots, cut into thin strips	3 small carrots, cut into thin strips
1 green pepper, cored, seeded and sliced	1 green pepper, seeded and sliced
1 × 284 g/10 oz can pineapple pieces, drained	1 can (8 oz) pineapple chunks, drained

Heat the oil in the wok. Add the pork and stir-fry for 5 minutes. Stir in the soy sauce, sherry and sugar. Add the carrots, green pepper and pineapple and stir-fry for about 5 minutes. Serve with boiled rice or noodles.
Serves 3 to 4

Pork Chop Suey

METRIC/IMPERIAL	AMERICAN
3 tablespoons oil	3 tablespoons oil
1 egg, beaten	1 egg, beaten
1 bunch spring onions, cut into 5 cm/2 inch pieces	1 bunch scallions, cut into 2 inch pieces
1 slice root ginger, peeled and finely chopped	1 slice ginger root, peeled and finely chopped
1 clove garlic, crushed	1 clove garlic, crushed
2 tablespoons soy sauce	2 tablespoons soy sauce
2 tablespoons tomato purée	2 tablespoons tomato paste
6 tablespoons chicken stock	6 tablespoons chicken stock or broth
freshly ground pepper	freshly ground pepper
225 g/8 oz cooked pork, cut into thin strips	½ lb cooked pork, cut into thin strips (about 1½ cups)
300 g/10 oz bean sprouts	5 cups bean sprouts

Heat 1 tablespoon of the oil in the wok. Add the beaten egg, swirl round the sides and fry into a thin omelette. Remove and keep warm. Heat the remaining oil in the wok. Add the spring onions (scallions), ginger and garlic and stir-fry for a few minutes. Add the soy sauce, tomato purée (paste), chicken stock and pepper to taste, and mix well. Add the pork and bean sprouts and cook gently for about 8 minutes. Cut the omelette into strips. Serve the chop suey garnished with the omelette strips.
Serves 3 to 4

Pork and Pineapple Stir-Fry
(Photograph: Mazola Pure Corn Oil)

Pork Spring Rolls

METRIC/IMPERIAL	AMERICAN
1-2 tablespoons oil	1-2 tablespoons oil
2 spring onions, chopped	2 scallions, chopped
1 stick celery, chopped	1 stalk celery, chopped
75 g/3 oz cooked pork, chopped	½ cup chopped cooked pork
50 g/2 oz peeled prawns	⅓ cup shelled shrimp
3 canned water chestnuts, chopped	3 canned water chestnuts, chopped
50 g/2 oz bean sprouts	1 cup bean sprouts
75 g/3 oz cooked long-grain rice	½ cup cooked long-grain rice
2 teaspoons cornflour	2 teaspoons cornstarch
2 teaspoons soy sauce	2 teaspoons soy sauce
1 tablespoon sherry	1 tablespoon sherry
8 ready made pancakes, cooked on one side only in the wok	8 ready made crêpes, cooked on one side only in the wok
1 egg, beaten	1 egg, beaten
oil for deep frying	oil for deep frying

Heat the oil in the wok. Add the spring onions (scallions) and celery and stir-fry until soft. Add the pork, prawns (shrimp), water chestnuts, bean sprouts and rice, and stir-fry lightly for a few minutes. Blend the cornflour (cornstarch) with the soy sauce and sherry. Add to the wok and cook until the sauce has thickened, stirring continuously.

Spoon equal quantities of the filling in the centre of the cooked side of each pancake (crêpe). Brush the edges with beaten egg and fold into neat parcels. Seal all the edges with egg. Leave, seam side down, in a cool place for 10 minutes to set.

Wipe out or wash the wok. Heat enough oil in the wok for deep frying. When a temperature of 190°C/375°F is reached, fry the rolls for about 4 minutes or until crisp and golden on all sides. Drain well on kitchen paper towels and serve hot with savoury rice.
Serves 4

Pork in Soured Cream Sauce

METRIC/IMPERIAL	AMERICAN
450 g/1 lb pork fillet, cut into strips	1 lb pork tenderloin, cut into strips
grated rind and juice of 1 large lemon	grated rind and juice of 1 large lemon
1 tablespoon oil	1 tablespoon oil
25 g/1 oz butter	2 tablespoons butter
1 medium onion, finely chopped	1 medium-size onion, finely chopped
1 clove garlic, crushed	1 clove garlic, crushed
1 tablespoon flour	1 tablespoon flour
150 ml/¼ pint dry white wine	⅔ cup dry white wine
300 ml/½ pint soured cream	1¼ cups sour cream
salt and freshly ground pepper	salt and freshly ground pepper
1 tablespoon chopped parsley	1 tablespoon chopped parsley

Marinate the pork in the lemon rind and juice for at least 8 hours. Drain and dry the meat, reserving the marinade.

Heat the oil and butter in the wok. Add the onion and garlic and stir-fry for 3 minutes or until soft. Add the meat and stir-fry for 5 minutes. Push the onion and meat to one side. Sprinkle the flour into the bottom of the wok and stir well. Add the wine, marinade, soured cream and salt and pepper to taste and stir until smooth. Mix the meat, onion and parsley into the cream sauce. Cover with the lid and cook gently for about 5 minutes. Serve with boiled new potatoes and a green salad.
Serves 4

Spicy Pork Stroganoff

METRIC/IMPERIAL	AMERICAN
3 tablespoons oil	3 tablespoons oil
1 kg/2 lb pork fillet, thinly sliced	2 lb pork tenderloin, thinly sliced
1 large onion, chopped	1 large onion, chopped
2 tablespoons paprika	2 tablespoons paprika
2 teaspoons dry mustard	2 teaspoons dry mustard
150 ml/¼ pint stock	⅔ cup stock or broth
2 tablespoons tomato purée	2 tablespoons tomato paste
150 ml/¼ pint soured cream	⅔ cup sour cream
salt and freshly ground pepper	salt and freshly ground pepper

Heat the oil in the wok. Add the pork and onion and stir-fry for about 5 minutes or until tender but not browned. Sprinkle on the paprika and mustard and add the stock and tomato purée (paste). Stir until well blended. Cover with the lid and simmer gently for 12 to 15 minutes. Stir in the soured cream, reheat without boiling and season to taste with salt and pepper. Serve at once with buttered noodles and a salad.
Serves 4 to 5

Braised Knuckle (Hock) of Pork

METRIC/IMPERIAL	AMERICAN
1 × 1.5 kg/3 lb knuckle of pork, cleaned	1 (3 lb) pork hock, cleaned
450 ml/¾ pint good stock	2 cups stock or broth
4 tablespoons soy sauce	¼ cup soy sauce
4 tablespoons dry sherry	¼ cup dry sherry
1 tablespoon five spice powder	1 tablespoon five spice powder
3 tablespoons sugar	3 tablespoons sugar

Place the pork in a casserole dish (one which will fit in your wok). Pour in the stock, soy sauce, sherry, spice and sugar. Turn the pork in this marinade. Place the lid on the casserole and put into the wok with 9 cm/3½ inches boiling water to come up the sides of the dish. Cover with the wok lid and steam the pork over the simmering water for 3 to 4 hours or until tender. Turn the pork in the marinade every hour. Top up with boiling water as necessary. The meat and fat will become rich and tender.
Serves 4 to 6

For a complete Chinese meal, serve with Beef Chow Mein (page 16), Steamed Whole Fish (page 7), Lettuce in Oyster Sauce (page 56) and lychees for 6 people.
Illustrated on page 6

Pork Balls with Lettuce over Rice

METRIC/IMPERIAL	AMERICAN
225 g/8 oz lean pork	½ lb lean pork
100 g/4 oz water chestnuts	¼ lb water chestnuts
salt and freshly ground pepper	salt and freshly ground pepper
1 egg, beaten	1 egg, beaten
1 tablespoon cornflour	1 tablespoon cornstarch
1 tablespoon oil	1 tablespoon oil
350 g/12 oz lettuce, shredded	3 cups shredded lettuce
½ bunch celery, chopped	½ head celery, chopped
300 ml/½ pint water	1¼ cups water
1 tablespoon soy sauce	1 tablespoon soy sauce

Finely mince (grind) the pork and water chestnuts together. Add salt and pepper to taste, the beaten egg and cornflour (cornstarch). Mix until evenly blended. Shape the mixture into walnut-size balls.

Heat the oil in the wok. Add the lettuce and celery and stir-fry for 2 to 3 minutes. Add the water and soy sauce and bring to the boil. Place the meat balls on top of the vegetables. Cover with the lid and cook for about 15 minutes or until the meat balls are tender.

Serve the meat balls and vegetables on a bed of rice.
Serves 4

Sausage, Bacon and Beans

METRIC/IMPERIAL	AMERICAN
25 g/1 oz lard	2 tablespoons shortening
450 g/1 lb tiny cocktail pork sausages	1 lb tiny cocktail sausages
1 large onion, thinly sliced	1 large onion, thinly sliced
4 rashers streaky bacon, rinds removed and chopped	4 slices bacon, chopped
25 g/1 oz flour	¼ cup flour
300 ml/½ pint stock	1¼ cups stock or broth
100 g/4 oz mushrooms, sliced	1 cup sliced mushrooms
1 tablespoon tomato purée	1 tablespoon tomato paste
salt and freshly ground pepper	salt and freshly ground pepper
1 × 225 g/8 oz can baked beans in tomato sauce	1 can (8 oz) baked beans in tomato sauce

Heat the lard (shortening) in the wok. Add the sausages and fry for about 8 minutes or until browned on all sides. Remove and keep warm. Add the onion and bacon to the wok and stir-fry for about 5 minutes or until lightly browned. Stir in the flour, then add the stock, mushrooms, tomato purée (paste) and salt and pepper to taste. Cook for 2 minutes, stirring. Return the sausages to the wok and add the baked beans. Cover with the lid and cook for about 5 minutes. Serve with mashed potatoes.
Serves 4

Peking-Style Pork

METRIC/IMPERIAL	AMERICAN
450 g/1 lb pork fillet, cut into 1 cm/½ inch cubes	1 lb pork tenderloin, cut into ½ inch cubes
2 tablespoons vegetable oil	2 tablespoons vegetable oil
100 g/4 oz button mushrooms	1 cup button mushrooms
½ red pepper, cored, seeded and cut in squares	½ red pepper, seeded and cut in squares
¼ cucumber, cubed	¼ cucumber, cubed
2 teaspoons sesame oil	2 teaspoons sesame oil
2 teaspoons sesame paste	2 teaspoons sesame paste
2 teaspoons soy sauce	2 teaspoons soy sauce
2 teaspoons tomato purée	2 teaspoons tomato paste
2 teaspoons hoisin sauce	2 teaspoons hoisin sauce
1 tablespoon dry sherry	1 tablespoon pale dry sherry
1 teaspoon chilli sauce	1 teaspoon chili sauce

Heat the oil in the wok and stir-fry the pork until browned all over. Move it to one side. Add the mushrooms and stir-fry in the hot oil for 1 minute. Add the red pepper and cucumber and stir-fry over a high heat for 1½ minutes. Push to one side of the wok.

Add the sesame oil to the centre of the pan with the remaining ingredients and enough water to make a smooth sauce. Stir over a high heat until thoroughly blended and simmering. Stir in the pork and vegetables from around the side and mix in well. Stir-fry for 1 minute and serve immediately.
Serves 4

Clockwise from front: Peking-Style Pork;
Chicken with Cashew Nuts (page 42);
Stir-Fried Vegetable Rice (page 49); Beef with
Oyster Sauce (page 17)
(Photograph: US Rice Council)

Pork with Aubergine (Eggplant)

METRIC/IMPERIAL	AMERICAN
1 aubergine, sliced	1 eggplant, sliced
salt	salt
350 g/12 oz minced pork	¾ lb ground pork
1 tablespoon soy sauce	1 tablespoon soy sauce
2 tablespoons oil	2 tablespoons oil
1 onion, thinly sliced	1 onion, thinly sliced
1 × 425 g/15 oz can tomatoes	1 can (16 oz) tomatoes
2 teaspoons sugar	2 teaspoons sugar

Sprinkle the aubergine (eggplant) with salt. Leave for 30 minutes, then rinse and pat dry with kitchen paper towels. Sprinkle the pork with a little salt and the soy sauce.

Heat the oil in the wok. Add the pork and onion and stir-fry for about 5 minutes or until browned. Stir in the aubergine (eggplant), undrained tomatoes and sugar. Cover with the lid and cook for about 15 minutes, stirring occasionally, until the aubergine (eggplant) is cooked.
Serves 3 to 4

Crunchy Bacon and Mushroom Salad

METRIC/IMPERIAL	AMERICAN
50 g/2 oz butter	¼ cup butter
2 tablespoons oil	2 tablespoons oil
4 slices white bread, crusts removed and cut into 1 cm/½ inch cubes	4 slices white bread, crusts removed and cut into ½ inch cubes
6 rashers streaky bacon, rinds removed and roughly chopped	6 slices bacon, roughly chopped
225 g/8 oz mushrooms, sliced	2 cups sliced mushrooms
½ medium onion, grated	½ medium-size onion, grated
pinch of dry mustard	pinch of dry mustard
salt and freshly ground pepper	salt and freshly ground pepper
4-5 tablespoons vinaigrette dressing	4-5 tablespoons Italian dressing

Heat the butter and oil in the wok. Fry the cubes of bread until crisp and golden. Remove and drain on kitchen paper towels. Add the bacon to the wok and lightly fry until just crisp. Remove and drain. Stir-fry the mushrooms in the remaining fat until softened. Remove and drain.

Place the mushrooms in a salad bowl and add the grated onion, mustard and salt and pepper to taste. Toss in the dressing. Cool, then add the fried bread cubes and bacon, and serve.
Serves 4

Minced (Ground) Pork with Noodles

METRIC/IMPERIAL	AMERICAN
3 tablespoons oil	3 tablespoons oil
1 large onion, chopped	1 large onion, chopped
450 g/1 lb minced pork	1 lb ground pork
2 tablespoons yellow bean sauce	2 tablespoons yellow bean sauce
1 tablespoon light soy sauce	1 tablespoon light soy sauce
1 tablespoon sugar	1 tablespoon sugar
1 tablespoon cornflour	1 tablespoon cornstarch
4 tablespoons stock	¼ cup stock or broth
about 225 g/8 oz Chinese egg noodles	about ½ lb Chinese egg noodles
chopped cucumber and spring onions to garnish	chopped cucumber and scallions for garnish

Heat the oil in the wok. Add the onion and pork and stir-fry for about 5 minutes. Add the bean sauce, soy sauce and sugar and cook for a further few minutes. Blend the cornflour (cornstarch) into the stock and add. Stir until thickened. Simmer gently for 15 to 20 minutes.

Cook the noodles in boiling salted water for 5 to 6 minutes, then drain. Pour the pork sauce over the noodles and garnish with cucumber and spring onions (scallions).
Serves 4

Deep-Fried Pork in Sweet and Sour Sauce

METRIC/IMPERIAL	AMERICAN
25 g/1 oz cornflour	¼ cup cornstarch
1 teaspoon salt	1 teaspoon salt
pinch of baking powder	pinch of baking powder
225 g/8 oz lean pork, cubed	½ lb lean pork, cubed
1 egg, beaten	1 egg, beaten
oil for deep frying	oil for deep frying
1 jar Hong Kong sweet and sour stir-fry sauce, heated	1 jar Hong Kong sweet and sour stir-fry sauce, heated

Mix the cornflour (cornstarch), salt and baking powder together. Toss the pork in this mixture, then dip in the beaten egg. Toss again in the cornflour (cornstarch) mixture.

Heat enough oil in the wok for deep frying. When a temperature of 190°C/375°F is reached, fry the pork for 2 to 3 minutes, in several batches. Re-crisp the pork in the oil, then drain on kitchen paper towels, pour over the heated sauce and serve.

Serves 3 to 4

For a complete Chinese meal, serve with soup, fried rice, Celery in Pearl Sauce (page 58), Chicken in Yellow Bean Sauce (page 42) and a fruit salad, for 6 people.

Illustrated on page 43

Honeyed Spare Ribs

METRIC/IMPERIAL	AMERICAN
1 kg/2 lb pork spare ribs	2 lb pork spare ribs
3 tablespoons clear honey	3 tablespoons clear honey
5 tablespoons tomato ketchup	5 tablespoons tomato ketchup
2 tablespoons soy sauce	2 tablespoons soy sauce
3 tablespoons vinegar	3 tablespoons vinegar
1 tablespoon tomato purée	1 tablespoon tomato paste
about 200 ml/⅓ pint stock	about 1 cup stock or broth
salt and freshly ground pepper	salt and freshly ground pepper

Ask your butcher to chop the ribs into 7.5 cm/3 inch lengths, dividing between each bone. Put the ribs into a heatproof dish which will fit inside the wok. Mix the remaining ingredients together, with salt and pepper to taste, and pour over the ribs. Leave to marinate in the refrigerator for at least 2 hours, turning over in the sauce from time to time.

Place the dish of spare ribs on the steaming rack in the wok over simmering water. Cover with the lid and steam for about 1 hour or until tender, turning the spare ribs in the sauce several times during cooking. Top up with boiling water as necessary. If liked, the sauce can be thickened with 1 tablespoon cornflour (cornstarch).

Serves 4

Poultry Dishes

Duck with Almonds

METRIC/IMPERIAL	AMERICAN
1 × 2-2.5 kg/4½-5 lb duckling	1 (4½-5 lb) duck
salt	salt
1 large onion, chopped	1 large onion, chopped
3 sticks celery, chopped	3 stalks celery, chopped
100 g/4 oz mushrooms, thinly sliced	1 cup thinly sliced mushrooms
1 × 156 g/5½ oz can water chestnuts, drained and sliced	1 can (5½ oz) water chestnuts, drained and sliced
2 tablespoons cornflour	2 tablespoons cornstarch
1 teaspoon ground ginger	1 teaspoon ground ginger
2 tablespoons soy sauce	2 tablespoons soy sauce
450 ml/¾ pint duckling giblet stock	2 cups duck giblet stock
50 g/2 oz toasted almonds	½ cup toasted almonds
celery leaves or spring onion curls to garnish	celery leaves or scallion curls for garnish

Thoroughly dry the duck inside and out with kitchen paper towels. Prick the skin, sprinkle well with salt, then place on a rack in a roasting tin. Roast in a preheated moderate oven (180°C/350°F, Gas Mark 4), allowing 30 minutes per 450 g/1 lb. Allow the duck to cool, and reserve 1 tablespoon of the dripping in the roasting tin.

Remove the skin from the duck and cut into strips. Remove the duck meat from the carcass, cut into strips and keep separately. Heat the wok, add the strips of duck skin and cook until crisp and brown. Drain well over the pan and keep on one side.

Add the reserved dripping to the wok with the onion and celery and fry for 2 to 3 minutes until tender. Add the mushrooms and continue cooking for 4 to 5 minutes. Stir in the water chestnuts and duck meat and continue cooking until heated through. Push the ingredients up the sides of the wok.

Blend the cornflour (cornstarch) and ginger with the soy sauce and stock, pour into the wok and stir until the sauce thickens. Mix in the duck and vegetables from the sides of the pan. Add the toasted almonds and stir well.

Serve in a border of cooked rice, garnished with the crisp duck skin and celery leaves or spring onion (scallion) curls.
Serves 4

Duck with Almonds
(Photograph: British Duck Advisory Bureau)

Chicken with Deep-Fried Noodles

METRIC/IMPERIAL	AMERICAN
225 g/8 oz Chinese egg noodles	½ lb Chinese egg noodles
3 tablespoon oil	3 tablespoons oil
1½ tablespoons soy sauce	1½ tablespoons soy sauce
½ teaspoon sugar	½ teaspoon sugar
225 g/8 oz cooked chicken meat, cut into thin strips	½ lb cooked chicken meat, cut into thin strips (about 1½ cups)
3 spring onions, sliced diagonally into 1 cm/½ inch pieces	3 scallions, sliced diagonally into ½ inch pieces
2.5 cm/1 inch piece root ginger, peeled and thinly sliced	1 inch piece ginger root, peeled and thinly sliced
1 carrot, thinly sliced	1 carrot, thinly sliced
2 sticks celery, thinly sliced	2 stalks celery, thinly sliced
1 × 200 g/7 oz can bamboo shoots, drained and sliced	1 can (8 oz) bamboo shoots, drained and sliced
50 g/2 oz mushrooms, sliced	½ cup sliced mushrooms
1 teaspoon cornflour	1 teaspoon cornstarch
3 tablespoons chicken stock	3 tablespoons chicken stock or broth
oil for deep frying	oil for deep frying

Cook the noodles in boiling salted water in a saucepan for 5 minutes. Rinse and drain. Stir in 1 tablespoon of the oil.

Mix together the soy sauce and sugar. Marinate the chicken and spring onions (scallions) in this mixture for 20 minutes.

Meanwhile, heat the remaining oil in the wok. Add the ginger and cook for 2 minutes. Add the carrot and celery and stir-fry for 5 minutes. Add the bamboo shoots and mushrooms and stir-fry for a further 2 minutes. Mix together the cornflour (cornstarch) and chicken stock and stir into the vegetables. Stir in the chicken and the marinade. Cook for a further 5 minutes to heat through. Transfer to a heated serving dish and keep warm.

Wipe out or wash the wok. Heat enough oil in the wok for deep frying. When a temperature of 190°C/375°F is reached, fry the noodles in four batches, each for 3 to 5 minutes or until crisp and golden. Drain on kitchen paper towels. Serve with the chicken.
Serves 4

Chicken with Pineapple and Bean Sprouts

METRIC/IMPERIAL	AMERICAN
3 tablespoons oil	3 tablespoons oil
1 medium onion, roughly chopped	1 medium-size onion, roughly chopped
1 medium carrot, grated	1 medium-size carrot, grated
1 small green pepper, cored, seeded and chopped	1 small green pepper, seeded and chopped
100 g/4 oz mushrooms, sliced if large	¼ lb mushrooms, sliced if large
1 tablespoon cornflour	1 tablespoon cornstarch
2 tablespoons water	2 tablespoons water
450 g/1 lb cooked chicken meat, cubed	3 cups cubed cooked chicken meat
2 tablespoons sugar	2 tablespoons sugar
1 tablespoon soy sauce	1 tablespoon soy sauce
3 tablespoons wine vinegar	3 tablespoons wine vinegar
75 ml/2½ fl oz chicken stock	⅓ cup chicken stock or broth
1 tablespoon tomato purée	1 tablespoon tomato paste
1 × 225 g/8 oz can pineapple pieces	1 can (8 oz) pineapple chunks
1 × 265 g/9½ oz can bean sprouts	1 can (8 oz) bean sprouts
25 g/1 oz almonds, split and toasted	¼ cup split and toasted almonds

Heat the oil in the wok. Add the onion, carrot, green pepper and mushrooms and stir-fry for 3 minutes. Blend the cornflour (cornstarch) with the water and stir into the vegetables. Add the chicken, sugar, soy sauce, vinegar, stock, tomato purée (paste) and undrained pineapple. Simmer gently for 15 minutes, stirring occasionally.

Meanwhile, heat the bean sprouts in a saucepan. Pour the chicken mixture on to a large heated dish and spoon the bean sprouts at each end. Sprinkle the almonds over the top. Serve with boiled rice.
Serves 4 to 6

Chicken with Peppers, Tomatoes and Olives

METRIC/IMPERIAL	AMERICAN
1 × 1.5 kg/3 lb chicken, cut into 8 pieces	1 (3 lb) broiler/fryer, cut into 8 pieces
salt and freshly ground pepper	salt and freshly ground pepper
3 tablespoons oil	3 tablespoons oil
2 large onions, chopped	2 large onions, chopped
2 cloves garlic, crushed	2 cloves garlic, crushed
1 medium green pepper, cored, seeded and cut into strips	1 medium-size green pepper, seeded and cut into strips
1 medium red pepper, cored, seeded and cut into strips	1 medium-size red pepper, seeded and cut into strips
50 g/2 oz smoked ham, finely chopped	¼ cup finely chopped cooked ham
1 × 425 g/15 oz can tomatoes	1 can (16 oz) tomatoes
8 stoned green olives, halved	8 pitted green olives, halved
8 stoned black olives, halved	8 pitted ripe olives, halved

Sprinkle the chicken pieces with a little salt and pepper. Heat the oil in the wok. Add the chicken pieces and fry for about 5 minutes until lightly browned on all sides. Remove from the wok. Add the onions, garlic and green and red peppers to the wok and stir-fry for about 5 minutes. Stir in the ham and undrained tomatoes and, over a fairly high heat, cook to reduce the liquid to a thickish sauce.

Return the chicken pieces to the wok, cover with the lid and simmer for 25 minutes or until the chicken is tender. Stir in the halved olives and check the seasoning. Serve with saffron rice.
Serves 4

Honeyed Chicken

METRIC/IMPERIAL	AMERICAN
4 tablespoons honey	¼ cup honey
1 teaspoon curry powder	1 teaspoon curry powder
½ teaspoon pepper	½ teaspoon pepper
1 teaspoon salt	1 teaspoon salt
pinch of ground allspice	pinch of ground allspice
50 g/2 oz raisins	⅓ cup raisins
1 lemon, thinly sliced	1 lemon, thinly sliced
1 × 1.5 kg/3 lb chicken, cut into 6-8 pieces	1 (3 lb) chicken, cut into 6-8 pieces
300 ml/½ pint water	1¼ cups water
3 tablespoons oil	3 tablespoons oil
300 ml/½ pint chicken stock	1¼ cups chicken stock or broth
chopped parsley to garnish	chopped parsley for garnish

Mix together 2 tablespoons of the honey with the curry powder, pepper, salt, allspice, raisins and lemon slices. Spread over the chicken pieces. Cover and leave to marinate, overnight if possible.

Drain the chicken pieces and set aside. Simmer the marinade with the water in a saucepan until the lemon is tender. Heat the oil in the wok. Add the remaining 2 tablespoons of honey and the chicken pieces. Fry until golden brown on all sides. Add the marinade mixture and stock and bring to the boil. Cover with the lid and simmer for about 30 minutes or until the chicken is tender. Adjust the seasoning, adding more honey if required. Garnish with parsley. This is excellent served with spinach and pitta bread.
Serves 4 to 6

Chicken with Orange Sauce

METRIC/IMPERIAL	AMERICAN
4 chicken breasts, cut into strips	4 chicken breasts, cut into strips
½ teaspoon salt	½ teaspoon salt
100 g/4 oz butter	½ cup butter
25 g/1 oz flour	¼ cup flour
2 tablespoons soft brow sugar	2 tablespoons light brown sugar
½ teaspoon ground ginger	½ teaspoon ground ginger
freshly ground pepper	freshly ground pepper
250 ml/8 fl oz unsweetened orange juice	1 cup unsweetened orange juice
250 ml/8 fl oz water	1 cup water
½ teaspoon Tabasco sauce	½ teaspoon hot pepper sauce
1 orange, cut into 1 cm/½ inch thick slices and each slice quartered	1 orange, cut into ½ inch thick slices and each slice quartered

Sprinkle the chicken with the salt. Heat the butter in the wok. Add the chicken and stir-fry until browned on all sides. Push to one side or remove from the wok. Stir the flour, brown sugar, ginger and pepper to taste into the butter in the wok until smooth. Slowly stir in the orange juice, water and Tabasco (hot pepper sauce). Cook, stirring, until the mixture thickens and comes to the boil. Reduce the heat.

Return the chicken to the wok and add the orange pieces. Simmer for about 10 minutes. Serve with buttered new potatoes and courgettes (zucchini).
Serves 4

Chicken in Yellow Bean Sauce

METRIC/IMPERIAL	AMERICAN
450 g/1 lb uncooked chicken meat, diced	3 cups diced uncooked chicken meat
4 tablespoons oil	¼ cup oil
3 tablespoons cornflour	3 tablespoons cornstarch
50 g/2 oz peanuts or cashew nuts	½ cup peanuts or cashew nuts
1 jar Peking yellow bean stir-fry sauce	1 jar Peking yellow bean stir-fry sauce

Rub the chicken with a little of the oil, then dust with the cornflour (cornstarch). Heat the remaining oil in the wok. Add the nuts and stir-fry until browned. Add the chicken and stir-fry for about 4 minutes. Stir in the sauce and heat through.
Serves 4

For an authentic Chinese meal, serve with soup, fried rice, Celery in Pearl Sauce (page 58), Deep-Fried Pork in Sweet and Sour Sauce (page 37) and a fruit salad, for 6 people.

Chicken with Cashew Nuts

METRIC/IMPERIAL	AMERICAN
150 ml/¼ pint oil	⅔ cup oil
100 g/4 oz cashew nuts	1 cup cashew nuts
450 g/1 lb uncooked chicken meat, shredded	1 lb uncooked chicken meat, shredded
50 g/2 oz root ginger, peeled and thinly sliced	½ cup peeled and thinly sliced ginger root
150 ml/¼ pint yellow bean stir-fry sauce	⅔ cup yellow bean stir-fry sauce
100 g/4 oz bean sprouts	2 cups bean sprouts

Heat the oil in the wok until hot. Add the cashew nuts and toss in the oil until browned. Remove with a slotted spoon and keep warm. Reheat the oil, add the chicken and fry briskly until cooked. Remove the wok from the heat and pour off any excess oil.

Add the ginger and stir-fry for 1 minute. Stir in the yellow bean sauce and bean sprouts and heat through. Lightly stir in the cashew nuts and serve on a warmed plate.
Serves 4
Illustrated on page 35

Chicken in Yellow Bean Sauce; Deep-Fried Pork in Sweet and Sour Sauce (page 37); Celery in Pearl Sauce (page 58), served with soup, fried rice and fruit salad (Photograph: J A Sharwood Co Ltd)

Chicken in Cream Sauce

METRIC/IMPERIAL	AMERICAN
3 tablespoons oil	3 tablespoons oil
225 g/8 oz onion, chopped	2 cups chopped onion
1 kg/2 lb uncooked chicken meat, cut into thin strips	2 lb uncooked chicken meat, cut into thin strips
2 tablespoons tomato purée	2 tablespoons tomato paste
150 ml/¼ pint double cream	⅔ cup heavy cream
150 ml/¼ pint soured cream	⅔ cup sour cream
3 tablespoons diced dill cucumber	3 tablespoons diced dill pickle
salt and freshly ground pepper	salt and freshly ground pepper

Heat the oil in the wok. Add the onion and chicken and stir-fry for about 8 minutes or until the chicken is cooked. Stir in the tomato purée (paste), creams, cucumber (dill pickle) and salt and pepper to taste. Heat through, without boiling, for 5 minutes. Serve with rice.
Serves 6

Fried Chicken with Pineapple

METRIC/IMPERIAL	AMERICAN
1 tablespoon oil	1 tablespoon oil
1 × 425 g/15 oz can pineapple, drained and cut into pieces	1 can (16 oz) pineapple, drained and cut into pieces
350 g/12 oz uncooked chicken meat, thinly sliced	¾ lb uncooked chicken meat, thinly sliced
2 tablespoons pineapple juice	2 tablespoons pineapple juice
6 tablespoons chicken stock	6 tablespoons chicken stock or broth
1 tablespoon cornflour	1 tablespoon cornstarch
2 tablespoons sherry	2 tablespoons sherry
1 tablespoon soy sauce	1 tablespoon soy sauce
1 teaspoon brown sugar	1 teaspoon brown sugar
1 teaspoon pure sesame oil	1 teaspoon pure sesame oil
75 g/3 oz blanched almonds	¾ cup blanched almonds

Heat the oil in the wok. Add the pineapple and fry for 2 to 3 minutes. Add the chicken and stir-fry for about 2 minutes. Stir in the pineapple juice and stock and simmer for 5 minutes. Mix the cornflour (cornstarch) to a smooth paste with the sherry, soy sauce and brown sugar. Add to the chicken and stir until slightly thickened. Transfer to a heated serving dish and sprinkle with the sesame oil and almonds. Serve with fried rice.
Serves 4

Saucy Chicken

METRIC/IMPERIAL	AMERICAN
1 tablespoon oil	1 tablespoon oil
6 shallots or small onions, chopped	6 shallots or pearl onions, chopped
150 ml/¼ pint unsweetened orange juice	⅔ cup unsweetened orange juice
2 tablespoons tomato ketchup	2 tablespoons tomato ketchup
1 tablespoon cider or wine vinegar	1 tablespoon cider or wine vinegar
1 teaspoon brown sugar	1 teaspoon brown sugar
1 teaspoon Worcestershire sauce	1 teaspoon Worcestershire sauce
salt and freshly ground pepper	salt and freshly ground pepper
2 teaspoons cornflour	2 teaspoons cornstarch
1 tablespoon water	1 tablespoon water
450 g/1 lb cooked chicken meat, diced	3 cups diced cooked chicken meat
2 teaspoons chopped parsley to garnish	2 teaspoons chopped parsley for garnish

Heat the oil in the wok. Add the shallots or onions and stir-fry for 3 minutes. Stir in the orange juice, tomato ketchup, vinegar, brown sugar, Worcestershire sauce and salt and pepper to taste. Cover with the lid and simmer for about 10 minutes.

Blend the cornflour (cornstarch) with the water and add to the wok. Stir until the sauce begins to thicken. Add the chicken meat and heat through gently. Garnish with the chopped parsley.
Serves 4

Sweet and Sour Chicken

METRIC/IMPERIAL	AMERICAN
3 tablespoons oil	3 tablespoons oil
450 g/1 lb uncooked chicken meat, cut into strips	1 lb uncooked chicken meat, cut into strips
1 small onion, chopped	1 small onion, chopped
½ small green pepper, cored, seeded and thinly sliced	½ small green pepper, seeded and thinly sliced
1 carrot, cut into thin strips	1 carrot, cut into thin strips
450 ml/¾ pint + 2 tablespoons water	2 cups + 2 tablespoons water
3 tablespoons tomato ketchup	3 tablespoons tomato ketchup
25 g/1 oz sugar	2 tablespoons sugar
2 canned pineapple rings, roughly chopped	2 canned pinapple rings, roughly chopped
2 tablespoons syrup from can of pineapple	2 tablespoons syrup from can of pineapple
juice of ½ lemon	juice of ½ lemon
2 teaspoons malt vinegar	2 teaspoons vinegar
1 tablespoon cornflour	1 tablespoon cornstarch

Heat 2 tablespoons of the oil in the wok. Add the chicken strips and stir-fry for about 8 minutes or until tender. Remove and keep warm. Heat the remaining oil in the wok. Add the onion, green pepper and carrot and stir-fry for about 5 minutes or until the onion is soft but not brown. Stir in 450 ml/¾ pint (2 cups) of the water, the ketchup, sugar, pineapple, pineapple syrup, lemon juice and vinegar. Bring to the boil and simmer for about 10 minutes or until the sauce is reduced by almost half.

Return the chicken to the wok. Blend the cornflour (cornstarch) with the remaining water and stir into the sauce. Cook, stirring, for a few minutes until the sauce is thickened.
Serves 4

Spanish Chicken

METRIC/IMPERIAL	AMERICAN
1 × 1.5 kg/3½ lb chicken, cut into 8 pieces	1 (3½ lb) broiler-fryer, cut into 8 pieces
salt	salt
4 tablespoons oil	¼ cup oil
1 large onion, chopped	1 large onion, chopped
1 clove garlic, crushed	1 clove garlic, crushed
1 green pepper, cored, seeded and chopped	1 green pepper, seeded and chopped
1 × 425 g/15 oz can tomatoes	1 can (16 oz) tomatoes
4 tablespoons sherry	¼ cup sherry
½ teaspoon paprika	½ teaspoon paprika
2 whole cloves	2 whole cloves
1 bay leaf	1 bay leaf
150 ml/¼ pint water	⅔ cup water
freshly ground pepper	freshly ground pepper
3 courgettes, sliced	3 zucchini, sliced
1 large aubergine, cubed	1 large eggplant, cubed

Sprinkle the chicken pieces with salt. Heat the oil in the wok. Add the chicken pieces and fry for about 5 minutes or until browned on all sides. Remove from the wok. Add the onion, garlic and green pepper to the wok and stir-fry for 5 minutes. Add the chicken, undrained tomatoes, sherry, paprika, cloves, bay leaf, water and pepper to taste. Cover with the lid and simmer for 30 minutes. Add the courgettes (zucchini) and aubergine (eggplant), replace the lid and simmer for a further 15 minutes or until the chicken is tender. Discard the bay leaf before serving.
Serves 4

Rice & Egg Dishes

Mixed Seafood Rice Stick Noodles

METRIC/IMPERIAL

450 g/1 lb rice stick
    noodles
3-4 tablespoons oil
2 onions, thinly sliced
3 slices root ginger,
    peeled and
    shredded
3 rashers bacon,
    shredded
4 large dried Chinese
    mushrooms,
    soaked for 20
    minutes, drained,
    stemmed and
    shredded
1½ tablespoons dried
    shrimps, soaked for
    15 minutes and
    drained
4-5 tablespoons fresh
    or canned clams
6 tablespoons stock
3 tablespoons soy
    sauce
1 teaspoon salt
25 g/1 oz lard
100-225 g/4-8 oz
    broccoli, separated
    into florets
4-5 tablespoons
    peeled prawns
100 g/4 oz fresh
    squid, shredded
2 tablespoons sherry

AMERICAN

1 lb rice sticks
3-4 tablespoons oil
2 onions, thinly sliced
3 slices ginger root,
    peeled and
    shredded
3 slices bacon,
    shredded
4 large dried Chinese
    mushrooms,
    soaked for 20
    minutes, drained,
    stemmed and
    shredded
1½ tablespoons dried
    shrimp, soaked for
    15 minutes and
    drained
¼ cup fresh or
    canned clams
6 tablespoons stock
    or broth
3 tablespoons soy
    sauce
1 teaspoon salt
2 tablespoons lard
¼-½ lb broccoli,
    separated into
    flowerettes
¼ cup shelled shrimp
¼ lb fresh squid,
    shredded
2 tablespoons pale
    dry sherry

Cook the noodles (rice sticks) in boiling water for 7 to 8 minutes. Drain and rinse in a colander under cold running water to wash away any excess starch.

Heat the oil in the wok. Add the onions, ginger, bacon, mushrooms, dried shrimps and clams and stir-fry for 3 minutes. Add half the stock, 2 tablespoons of the soy sauce and the salt. Continue to stir-fry for a further 1½ minutes. Add the noodles and mix well. Increase the heat to high and cook, stirring, for a further 3 to 4 minutes. Remove from the heat.

Melt the lard in another pan. Add the broccoli and stir-fry over high heat for 2 minutes. Add the remaining soy sauce and stock, the fresh prawns (shrimp) and squid. Stir-fry for 2 minutes. Sprinkle in the sherry and remove from the heat. Keep hot.

Return the noodle mixture to the heat and stir-fry for 30 seconds until heated through, then transfer to a large serving dish.

Garnish with the broccoli and fish mixture and serve hot.
Serves 4 to 6

Mixed Seafood Rice Stick Noodles

Pork Fried Rice

METRIC/IMPERIAL	AMERICAN
3 tablespoons oil	3 tablespoons oil
4 spring onions, chopped	4 scallions, chopped
¼ head Chinese cabbage, shredded	¼ head bok choy, shredded
750 g/1½ lb cooked long-grain rice (225 g/8 oz uncooked)	4 cups cooked long-grain rice (1¼ cups uncooked)
1 tablespoon peeled and chopped root ginger	1 tablespoon peeled and chopped ginger root
225 g/8 oz cooked pork, diced	1 cup diced cooked pork
2 tablespoons soy sauce	2 tablespoons soy sauce
½ teaspoon sugar	½ teaspoon sugar
salt and freshly ground pepper	salt and freshly ground pepper
3 eggs, beaten	3 eggs, beaten
2 tablespoons chopped parsley	2 tablespoons chopped parsley

Heat the oil in the wok. Add the spring onions (scallions) and Chinese cabbage (bok choy) and stir-fry for 5 minutes. Add the rice and stir-fry for a further 5 minutes. Add the ginger, pork, soy sauce, sugar and salt and pepper to taste. Stir well and heat through. Make a well in the centre of the rice and pour in the eggs. Stir until partially scrambled, then gradually work in the rice until well mixed. Sprinkle with the parsley and serve.
Serves 4

Turkish Risotto

METRIC/IMPERIAL	AMERICAN
3 tablespoons oil	3 tablespoons oil
1 onion, chopped	1 onion, chopped
1 aubergine, peeled and sliced	1 eggplant, peeled and sliced
1 courgette, sliced	1 zucchini, sliced
350 g/12 oz long-grain rice	1¾ cups long-grain rice
900 ml/1½ pints hot stock	4 cups hot stock or broth
100 g/4 oz peeled prawns	⅔ cup shelled shrimp

Heat the oil in the wok. Add the onion and fry for 3 minutes. Add the aubergine (eggplant) and courgette (zucchini) and stir-fry for 5 minutes until soft. Remove the aubergine (eggplant) and courgette (zucchini) and keep warm. Add the rice to the wok and stir-fry for 1 to 2 minutes. Add the hot stock. Bring to the boil and stir once. Cover with the lid and simmer for 15 minutes or until the rice is tender and liquid absorbed. Add the prawns (shrimp), aubergine (eggplant) and courgette (zucchini) to the rice mixture. Cover and cook for a further 5 minutes.
Serves 4

Far Eastern Rice

METRIC/IMPERIAL	AMERICAN
1 tablespoon oil	1 tablespoon oil
450 g/1 lb minced beef	1 lb ground beef
1 onion, chopped	1 onion, chopped
225 g/8 oz long-grain rice	1¼ cups long-grain rice
600 ml/1 pint beef stock	2½ cups beef stock or broth
¼ teaspoon ground ginger	¼ teaspoon ground ginger
¼ teaspoon black pepper	¼ teaspoon black pepper
pinch of cayenne pepper	pinch of cayenne
1 × 200 g/7 oz can bean sprouts, drained	1 can (8 oz) bean sprouts, drained
1 × 200 g/7 oz can bamboo shoots, drained and sliced	1 can (8 oz) bamboo shoots, drained and sliced
soy sauce to taste	soy sauce to taste

Heat the oil in the wok. Add the minced (ground) beef and onion and stir-fry for 5 to 8 minutes or until browned. Add the rice and stir-fry for a few minutes longer. Pour in the stock and add the ginger, pepper and cayenne. Bring to the boil and stir once. Cover with the lid and simmer for 10 minutes. Add the bean sprouts and bamboo shoots. Replace the lid and cook for a further 5 minutes or until the rice is tender and liquid absorbed. Add soy sauce to taste and serve.
Serves 4

Risotto Portugal

METRIC/IMPERIAL	AMERICAN
3 tablespoons oil	3 tablespoons oil
1 smoked sausage, sliced	1 smoked sausage, sliced
1 onion, chopped	1 onion, chopped
1 green pepper, cored, seeded and cut into thin strips	1 green pepper, seeded and cut into thin strips
1 red pepper, cored, seeded and cut into thin strips	1 red pepper, seeded and cut into thin strips
2 tomatoes, skinned and diced	2 tomatoes, peeled and diced
350 g/12 oz long-grain rice	1¾ cups long-grain rice
750 ml/1½ pints hot stock	4 cups hot stock or broth

Heat 1 tablespoon of the oil in the wok. Add the sliced sausage and fry for about 3 minutes or until browned. Remove and keep warm. Heat the remaining oil in the wok. Add the onion and peppers and stir-fry for 3 to 4 minutes. Add the tomatoes and rice and stir-fry for a further 1 to 2 minutes. Add the hot stock. Bring to the boil and stir once. Cover with the lid and simmer for 15 minutes or until the rice is tender and liquid absorbed. Add the sausage, cover and cook for a further 5 minutes.
Serves 4

Stir-Fried Vegetable Rice

METRIC/IMPERIAL	AMERICAN
4 tablespoons oil	¼ cup oil
1 bunch of spring onions, chopped	1 bunch of scallions, chopped
2 cloves garlic, crushed	2 cloves garlic, chopped
750 g/1½ lb cooked long-grain rice (225 g/8 oz uncooked)	4 cups cooked long-grain rice (1¼ cups uncooked)
4 tablespoons soy sauce	¼ cup soy sauce
4 eggs	4 eggs
salt and freshly ground pepper	salt and freshly ground pepper
75 g/3 oz frozen peas, thawed	¾ cup frozen peas, thawed
75 g/3 oz sweetcorn kernels (optional)	½ cup whole kernel corn (optional)

Heat the oil in the wok. Add the spring onions (scallions) and garlic and stir-fry for 3 minutes. Add the cooked rice, stirring to combine. Mix the soy sauce, eggs and salt and pepper to taste together and beat well. Make a well in the centre of the rice and pour in the eggs. Stir until partially scrambled, then gradually work in the rice until well mixed. Add the peas and corn and cook for 2 minutes, stirring occasionally.
Serves 4
Illustrated on page 35

Prawn (Shrimp) Fried Rice

METRIC/IMPERIAL	AMERICAN
3 tablespoons oil	3 tablespoons oil
3 eggs, beaten	3 eggs, beaten
1 onion, chopped	1 onion, chopped
50 g/2 oz mushrooms, sliced	½ cup sliced mushrooms
750 g/1½ lb cooked long-grain rice (225 g/8 oz uncooked)	4 cups cooked long-grain rice (1¼ cups uncooked)
50 g/2 oz water chestnuts, sliced	¼ cup sliced water chestnuts
50 g/2 oz watercress, chopped	½ cup chopped watercress
2 tablespoons soy sauce	2 tablespoons soy sauce
½ teaspoon sugar	½ teaspoon sugar
225-350 g/8-12 oz peeled prawns	1⅓-2 cups shelled shrimp

Heat 1 tablespoon of the oil in the wok. Add the beaten eggs, swirl round the sides of the wok and fry on both sides. Remove the omelette, shred and keep warm.

Heat the remaining oil in the wok. Add the onion and fry for 3 minutes. Add the mushrooms and stir-fry for 2 minutes. Stir in the rice. Add the water chestnuts, watercress, soy sauce, sugar and prawns (shrimp), stir well and heat through thoroughly for about 5 minutes. Serve topped with the shredded omelette.
Serves 4

Mushroom and Nut Pilaff

METRIC/IMPERIAL	AMERICAN
3 tablespoons oil	3 tablespoons oil
1 medium onion, sliced	1 medium-size onion, sliced
1 clove garlic, crushed	1 clove garlic, crushed
225 g/8 oz mushrooms, quartered	½ lb mushrooms, quartered
2 sticks celery, chopped	2 stalks celery, chopped
1 red pepper, cored, seeded and chopped	1 red pepper, seeded and chopped
1 green pepper, cored, seeded and chopped	1 green pepper, seeded and chopped
100 g/4 oz cashew nuts, chopped	1 cup chopped cashew nuts
1 tablespoon soy sauce	1 tablespoon soy sauce
225 g/8 oz brown rice, cooked	1¼ cups brown rice, cooked
salt and freshly ground pepper	salt and freshly ground pepper

Heat the oil in the wok. Add the onion and fry for about 5 minutes or until transparent. Add the garlic, mushrooms, celery, red and green peppers, nuts and soy sauce and stir-fry for 5 to 7 minutes. Add the cooked brown rice, check the seasoning and toss the pilaff together, stirring until heated through. Serve with green salad.
Serves 4

Chinese Stir-Fried Rice

METRIC/IMPERIAL	AMERICAN
2 eggs	2 eggs
2 tablespoons water	2 tablespoons water
1½ tablespoons soy sauce	1½ tablespoons soy sauce
5 tablespoons vegetable oil	5 tablespoons vegetable oil
75 g/3 oz cabanos sausage, thinly sliced	½ cup thinly sliced cabanos sausage
1 onion, sliced	1 onion, sliced
50 g/2 oz uncooked chicken meat, diced	¼ cup diced uncooked chicken meat
50 g/2 oz beef, cubed	¼ cup cubed beef
50 g/2 oz peeled prawns	½ cup shelled shrimp
50 g/2 oz frozen peas, thawed	⅓ cup peas
pinch of cayenne pepper	pinch of cayenne
pinch of ground ginger	pinch of ground ginger
225 g/8 oz long-grain rice, cooked	1 cup long-grain rice, cooked
salt and freshly ground pepper	salt and freshly ground pepper

First make an omelette: beat together the eggs water and 1 teaspoon of the soy sauce. Heat 1 tablespoon of the oil in a pan and pour in the egg mixture. Using a fork, push the set egg to the centre, allowing unset egg to run to the edges. When the omelette is set, fold into three and transfer to a plate. When cool, cut the omelette into thin strips.

Heat 2 tablespoons oil in the wok, add the sausage and onion and stir-fry for 2 minutes. Using a slotted spoon, remove and keep warm. Add the chicken and beef to the wok and stir-fry for 2 minutes, then add the prawns (shrimp) and peas and stir-fry for 1 minute; remove from the pan and keep warm.

Heat the remaining oil in the wok, then add the rest of the soy sauce, the cayenne pepper and ginger and when very hot, add the cold cooked rice. Reduce the heat to low and stir-fry for 6 to 8 minutes.

Stir in the meat and vegetables and heat through briskly. Season to taste with salt and pepper and serve garnished with the omelette strips.
Serves 4

Mushroom and Nut Pilaff
(Photograph: Mushroom Growers'
Association)

Triple Layer Omelette

METRIC/IMPERIAL	AMERICAN
6 eggs	6 eggs
2 teaspoons salt	2 teaspoons salt
about 4 tablespoons oil	about ¼ cup oil
100 g/4 oz cooked ham, chopped	½ cup chopped cooked ham
100 g/4 oz peeled prawns	⅔ cup shelled shrimp
2 spring onions, chopped	2 scallions, chopped
chopped spring onion to garnish	chopped scallion for garnish
Soy and ginger dip:	**Soy and ginger dip:**
3 tablespoons soy sauce	3 tablespoons soy sauce
1 tablespoon vinegar	1 tablespoon vinegar
2 tablespoons sugar	2 tablespoons sugar
1 spring onion, finely chopped	1 scallion, finely chopped
2 cloves garlic, crushed	2 cloves garlic, crushed
1 tablespoon pure sesame oil	1 tablespoon pure sesame oil
5 tablespoons oil	5 tablespoons oil
3 slices pickled ginger or peeled root ginger, minced	3 slices pickled ginger or peeled ginger root, minced

Mix the dip ingredients together. Beat the eggs with the salt. Heat about 1 tablespoon oil in the wok. Add the ham and stir-fry for 1 minute. Reduce the heat and pour in one-third of the beaten egg. Tilt the wok, swirl the egg around and leave to cook for about 2 minutes until set. Lift out the omelette and place on a heated serving dish.

Add about 1 tablespoon oil to the wok and stir-fry the prawns (shrimp) for 1 minute. Pour in half the remaining egg and cook the omelette in the same way as before. Lay the second omelette on top of the first. Repeat the process using the spring onions (scallions).

Serve the layered omelette, garnished with spring onion (scallion), with the dip.
Serves 3 to 4

For a complete Chinese meal, serve with soup, rice, Hot Tossed Salad (page 62), Quick-Fried Beef with Peppers (page 15) and fruit, for 6 people.
Illustrated on page 14

Eggs Choux-Fleurs

METRIC/IMPERIAL	AMERICAN
2 tablespoons oil	2 tablespoons oil
25 g/1 oz butter	2 tablespoons butter
1 medium cauliflower, broken into small florets	1 medium-size cauliflower, broken into small flowerettes
1 clove garlic, crushed	1 clove garlic, crushed
4 tablespoons water	¼ cup water
4 tomatoes, skinned and chopped	4 tomatoes, peeled and chopped
100 g/4 oz mushrooms, chopped	1 cup chopped mushrooms
salt and freshly ground pepper	salt and freshly ground pepper
4 eggs	4 eggs
50 g/2 oz cheese, grated	½ cup grated cheese

Heat the oil and butter in the wok. Add the cauliflower and garlic and stir-fry for 2 minutes. Add the water, cover with the lid and cook for 4 minutes, stirring occasionally. Add the tomatoes, mushrooms and salt and pepper to taste and cook for 5 minutes. Make spaces in the mixture, drop in the eggs and sprinkle with the cheese. Cook for 3 to 5 minutes or until the eggs are set. Serve hot with crispy rolls or French bread.
Serves 4

Courgette (Zucchini) and Bacon Scramble

METRIC/IMPERIAL	AMERICAN
1 tablespoon oil	1 tablespoon oil
1 onion, finely chopped	1 onion, finely chopped
8 rashers streaky bacon, rinds removed and chopped	8 slices bacon, chopped
4 courgettes, chopped	4 zucchini, chopped
4 tomatoes, skinned and chopped	4 tomatoes, peeled and chopped
8 eggs	8 eggs
salt and freshly ground pepper	salt and freshly ground pepper

Heat the oil in the wok. Add the onion and bacon and stir-fry for 3 to 5 minutes or until the bacon is cooked. Add the courgettes (zucchini) and tomatoes and cook for 8 to 10 minutes or until the courgettes (zucchini) are tender. Beat the eggs together, adding salt and pepper to taste. Pour on to the vegetable mixture and cook gently, stirring continuously, until the eggs are just scrambled. Serve with toast.
Serves 4

Egg Foo Yung

METRIC/IMPERIAL	AMERICAN
15 g/½ oz butter	1 tablespoon butter
2 tablespoons oil	2 tablespoons oil
1 small onion, finely chopped	1 small onion, finely chopped
100 g/4 oz bean sprouts	2 cups bean sprouts
50 g/2 oz cooked meat, cut into thin strips	½ cup cooked meat, cut into thin strips
4 eggs	4 eggs
1 tablespoon soy sauce	1 tablespoon soy sauce
salt and freshly ground pepper	salt and freshly ground pepper
2 tablespoons chopped spring onions	2 tablespoons chopped scallions

Heat the butter and 1 tablespoon of the oil in the wok. Add the onion, bean sprouts and meat and stir-fry for 3 minutes. Remove and cool. Beat the eggs, soy sauce and salt and pepper to taste together. Add the cooled stir-fried ingredients.

Heat 1 teaspoon of the remaining oil in the wok, if necessary. Pour in one-quarter of the egg mixture. Tilt the wok, swirl the egg around and cook until lightly browned underneath. Turn over and cook the other side until lightly browned. Remove and keep warm. Heat another teaspoon of oil in the wok and cook the second omelette. Repeat this procedure twice more. (The egg mixture may be cooked in two batches, making one omelette per person.) Sprinkle the finished omelettes with spring onions (scaltions).
Serves 2

Chilli Eggs

METRIC/IMPERIAL	AMERICAN
50 g/2 oz butter	¼ cup butter
2 tablespoons oil	2 tablespoons oil
1 onion, finely chopped	1 onion, finely chopped
1 red pepper, cored, seeded and chopped	1 red pepper, seeded and chopped
175 g/6 oz cooked chicken meat, chopped	¾ cup chopped cooked chicken meat
8 eggs	8 eggs
¼ teaspoon chilli powder	¼ teaspoon chili powder
a few drops of Tabasco sauce	a few drops of hot pepper sauce
1 teaspoon Worcestershire sauce	1 teaspoon Worcestershire sauce
salt and freshly ground pepper	salt and freshly ground pepper
4 slices of bread, cut into triangles	4 slices of bread, cut into triangles

Heat half the butter and oil in the wok. Add the onion and red pepper and stir-fry for 3 minutes. Add the chicken and stir-fry for a further 5 minutes. Beat the eggs with the chilli powder, Tabasco (hot pepper sauce), Worcestershire sauce and salt and pepper to taste. Reduce the heat and add the eggs to the wok. Cook, stirring continuously, until the eggs are scrambled. Transfer the mixture to heated serving plates.

Wipe out or wash the wok and heat the remaining butter and oil. Fry the bread triangles until golden and crisp on both sides. Drain and serve with the eggs.
Serves 4

Vegetable Dishes

Spiced Aubergines (Eggplants) and Tomatoes

METRIC/IMPERIAL	AMERICAN
175 g/6 oz clarified butter or 4 tablespoons oil	¾ cup clarified butter or ¼ cup oil
1 large onion, sliced	1 large onion, sliced
2 cloves garlic, sliced	2 cloves garlic, sliced
1 teaspoon ground coriander	1 teaspoon ground coriander
2.5 cm/1 inch cinnamon stick	1 inch cinnamon stick
1 teaspoon chilli powder	1 teaspoon chili powder
1 teaspoon salt	1 teaspoon salt
1 teaspoon pepper	1 teaspoon pepper
450 g/1 lb aubergines, cut into 2.5 cm/ 1 inch pieces	1 lb eggplant, cut into 1 inch pieces
450 g/1 lb tomatoes, cut into 2.5 cm/ 1 inch pieces	1 lb tomatoes, cut into 1 inch pieces
3 tablespoons tomato purée	3 tablespoons tomato paste
200 ml/⅓ pint water	1 cup water

Heat the butter or oil in the wok. Add the onion and garlic and fry until soft. Add the spices and seasonings and stir-fry for 3 minutes.

Add the aubergines (eggplant), tomatoes and tomato purée (paste) and toss gently to coat with the spice mixture.

Stir in the water and bring to the boil. Lower the heat and simmer for 25 to 30 minutes or until the aubergines (eggplant) are tender and the sauce is quite thick. Increase the heat to boil off any excess liquid, if necessary. Serve hot.
Serves 4

Clockwise from far left: Spiced Aubergines (Eggplants) and Tomatoes; Spiced Potatoes and Cauliflower; Spiced Spinach (page 56)

Spiced Potatoes and Cauliflower

METRIC/IMPERIAL	AMERICAN
175 g/6 oz clarified butter or 4 tablespoons oil	¾ cup clarified butter or ¼ cup oil
1 kg/2 lb potatoes, cut into 2.5 cm/1 inch pieces	2 lb potatoes, cut into 1 inch pieces
2 large onions, sliced	2 large onions, sliced
4 cloves garlic, sliced	4 cloves garlic, sliced
2 teaspoons chilli powder	2 teaspoons chili powder
1 teaspoon turmeric	1 teaspoon turmeric
1 teaspoon ground coriander	1 teaspoon ground coriander
2 teaspoons salt	2 teaspoons salt
½ teaspoon pepper	½ teaspoon pepper
1.2 litres/2 pints water	5 cups water
450 g/1 lb cauliflower florets	8 large cauliflower flowerettes
2 teaspoons garam masala	2 teaspoons garam masala

Heat the butter or oil in the wok. Add the potatoes and fry gently for exactly 1 minute. Remove from the wok with a slotted spoon and set aside.

Add the onions and garlic to the wok and fry until soft. Add the spices and seasonings, except the garam masala, and stir-fry for a further 3 minutes.

Return the potatoes to the wok, add the water and bring to the boil. Lower the heat and simmer for 10 minutes, then add the cauliflower. Simmer for a further 15 minutes or until the vegetables are tender and the sauce is thick.

Increase the heat to boil off any excess liquid if necessary. Stir in the garam masala and serve hot.
Serves 4

Bean Sprout Medley

METRIC/IMPERIAL	AMERICAN
3 tablespoons oil	3 tablespoons oil
2 eggs, beaten	2 eggs, beaten
1 onion, finely chopped	1 onion, finely chopped
1 clove garlic, crushed	1 clove garlic, crushed
1 red pepper, cored, seeded and sliced	1 red pepper, seeded and sliced
3 stics celery, chopped	3 stalks celery, chopped
100 g/4 oz mushrooms, sliced	1 cup sliced mushrooms
225 g/8 oz bean sprouts	4 cups bean sprouts
1 tablespoon soy sauce	1 tablespoon soy sauce
salt and freshly ground pepper	salt and freshly ground pepper

Heat 1 tablespoon of the oil in the wok. Add the beaten eggs, swirl round the sides and fry into a thin omelette. Remove and keep warm.

Heat the remaining oil in the wok. Add the onion, garlic, red pepper and celery and stir-fry for 5 minutes or until soft. Add the mushrooms and stir-fry for 3 to 5 minutes. Stir in the bean sprouts, soy sauce and salt and pepper to taste. Cover with the lid and cook for 2 minutes. Cut the omelette into strips or pieces and either stir into the mixture or use to garnish.
Serves 4

Spiced Spinach

METRIC/IMPERIAL	AMERICAN
50 g/2 oz clarified butter	¼ cup clarified butter
1 small onion, sliced	1 small onion, sliced
1 teaspoon garam masala	1 teaspoon garam masala
1 teaspoon salt	1 teaspoon salt
450 g/1 lb frozen whole leaf spinach	1 lb frozen whole leaf spinach

Heat the butter or oil in the wok. Add the onion and fry until soft. Add the garam masala and salt and stir-fry for a further 3 minutes. Add the frozen spinach and stir-fry for about 5 minutes until thawed and piping hot.
Serves 4
Illustrated on page 54

Lettuce in Oyster Sauce

METRIC/IMPERIAL	AMERICAN
2 Cos lettuces	2 heads Romaine lettuce
2 tablespoons oil	2 tablespoons oil
1 teaspoon pure sesame oil	1 teaspoon pure sesame oil
1 tablespoon soy sauce	1 tablespoon soy sauce
2 tablespoons good quality oyster sauce	2 tablespoons good quality oyster sauce

Tear the lettuce into individual leaves removing the core. Heat the oils in the wok. Add the lettuce and stir-fry for 1 minute. Add the soy sauce and oyster sauce, and toss for a further minute.
Serves 4
Illustrated on page 6

Stir-Fried Mange Tout (Snow Peas)

METRIC/IMPERIAL	AMERICAN
3 tablespoons oil	3 tablespoons oil
450 g/1 lb mange tout	1 lb snow peas
3 cloves garlic, crushed	3 cloves garlic, crushed
1 teaspoon salt	1 teaspoon salt
1 teaspoon sugar	1 teaspoon sugar

Heat the oil in the wok. Add the mange tout (snow peas), garlic, salt and sugar and stir-fry for 1 to 2 minutes or according to taste.
Serves 4

Stir-Fried Mushrooms and Chinese Cabbage (Bok Choy)

METRIC/IMPERIAL	AMERICAN
3 tablespoons peanut oil	3 tablespoons peanut oil
1 cm/½ inch piece root ginger, peeled and thinly sliced	½ inch piece ginger root, peeled and thinly sliced
1 small leek, white part only, thinly sliced	1 small leek, white part only, thinly sliced
1 small Chinese cabbage, white centre only, shredded	1 small head bok choy, white center only, shredded
450 g/1 lb button mushrooms, stalks removed	1 lb button mushrooms, stems removed
1 small spring onion, finely chopped	1 small scallion, finely chopped
2 teaspoons soy sauce	2 teaspoons soy sauce
1 tablespoon lemon juice	1 tablespoon lemon juice
large pinch of sea salt	large pinch of coarse sea salt
pinch of white pepper	pinch of white pepper

Heat the oil in the wok. Add the ginger and leek and stir-fry for 2 minutes. Add the cabbage (bok choy) and stir-fry for a further 2 minutes or until the cabbage is nearly cooked. Add the mushrooms and spring onion (scallion) and stir-fry for 2 minutes more. Mix in the soy sauce, lemon juice, salt and pepper. Serve with noodles.
Serves 4

Curried Vegetables

METRIC/IMPERIAL	AMERICAN
1 tablespoon turmeric	1 tablespoon turmeric
1 tablespoon curry powder or to taste	1 tablespoon curry powder or to taste
½ teaspoon salt	½ teaspoon salt
1 medium cauliflower, cut into florets	1 medium-size cauliflower, cut into flowerettes
6 tomatoes, skinned and sliced	6 tomatoes, peeled and sliced
6 potatoes, sliced	6 potatoes, sliced
100 g/4 oz peas	1 cup peas
100 g/4 oz green beans, sliced	½ cup sliced green beans
50 g/2 oz butter	¼ cup butter
2 onions, chopped	2 onions, chopped
1 clove garlic, crushed	1 clove garlic, crushed
300 ml/½ pint light stock	1¼ cups light stock or broth

Mix the turmeric, curry powder and salt together and use to sprinkle on the cauliflower, tomatoes, potatoes, peas and beans. Leave for 30 minutes.

Heat the butter in the wok. Add the onions and garlic and stir-fry for 3 minutes. Add the spiced vegetables and stir-fry for 5 minutes. Pour over the stock, cover with the lid and simmer for 10 to 15 minutes or until all the vegetables are just tender.
Serves 4

Celery in Pearl Sauce

METRIC/IMPERIAL	AMERICAN
1 tablespoon cornflour	1 tablespoon cornstarch
6 tablespoons good meat or bone stock	6 tablespoons meat or bone stock or broth
2 teaspoons salt	2 teaspoons salt
4 tablespoons oil	¼ cup oil
750 g/1½ lb celery or Chinese cabbage, sliced	1½ lb celery or bok choy, sliced

Blend the cornflour (cornstarch) with the stock and salt. Heat the oil in the wok. Add the celery and stir-fry for 2 minutes. Stir in the cornflour (cornstarch) sauce. Cover with the lid and braise for about 5 minutes.
Serves 4 to 6
Illustrated on page 43

Broccoli Fritters

METRIC/IMPERIAL	AMERICAN
450 g/1 lb broccoli, cut into 5 cm/2 inch pieces	1 lb broccoli, cut into 2 inch pieces
flour for coating	flour for coating
225 g/8 oz flour	2 cups flour
¼ teaspoon salt	¼ teaspoon salt
2 eggs, beaten	2 eggs, beaten
300 ml/½ pint milk	1¼ cups milk
oil for deep frying	oil for deep frying
grated Parmesan cheese to serve	grated Parmesan cheese to serve

Coat the broccoli in the flour. For the batter, sift the flour and salt into a bowl. Beat in the eggs and half the milk. Gradually beat in the remaining milk until smooth.

Heat about 10 cm/4 inches of oil in the wok. Test the temperature by dropping a little batter in the oil; if it rises immediately to the surface the oil is hot enough. Dip the pieces of broccoli in the batter and deep fry, a few at a time, for about 5 minutes or until golden brown and cooked. Drain on kitchen paper towels, sprinkle with Parmesan and serve immediately.
Serves 4

Egg Rolls

METRIC/IMPERIAL	AMERICAN
225 g/8 oz minced lean pork	½ lb ground lean pork
100 g/4 oz shelled prawns	½ cup shelled shrimp
1 tablespoon oil	1 tablespoon oil
2 spring onions, finely chopped	2 scallions, finely chopped
225 g/8 oz fresh or canned bean sprouts, drained	½ lb fresh or canned bean sprouts, drained
1 tablespoon soy sauce	1 tablespoon soy sauce
1 teaspoon salt	1 teaspoon salt
pinch of brown sugar	pinch of brown sugar
75 g/3 oz flour	¾ cup flour
300 ml/½ pint water	1¼ cups water
6 eggs, beaten	6 eggs, beaten
oil for deep frying	oil for deep frying
shredded spring onion to garnish	shredded scallion for garnish

Mix the pork and prawns (shrimp) together. Heat the oil in the wok. Add the pork mixture and fry for 2 minutes. Add the spring onions (scallions) and bean sprouts and stir-fry for a further 2 minutes or until the bean sprouts are tender. Stir in the soy sauce, salt and sugar. Pour into a bowl. Allow the wok to cool, then wipe it out.

Sift the flour into a bowl. Add the water and eggs and beat to a smooth batter. Heat a greased heavy-based frying pan (skillet). Pour in enough batter to make a thin pancake (crêpe) and cook on one side only. Transfer to a plate. Repeat with the remaining mixture.

Place some of the pork mixture in the centre of the cooked side of each pancake (crêpe). Fold the nearest edge over the filling, fold both sides into the centre, then roll up, sealing the last edge with a little water.

Heat enough oil in the wok for deep-frying. When a temperature of 180°C/350°F is reached, fry the rolls for about 10 minutes. Drain on absorbent kitchen paper. Serve hot.
Serves 4

Egg Rolls

Hot Tomato and Lettuce Salad

METRIC/IMPERIAL	AMERICAN
3 tablespoons oil	3 tablespoons oil
1 clove garlic, crushed	1 clove garlic, crushed
1 cucumber, thinly sliced	1 cucumber, thinly sliced
1 green pepper, cored, seeded and thinly sliced	1 green pepper, seeded and thinly sliced
2 tomatoes, cut into wedges	2 tomatoes, cut into wedges
8 lettuce leaves, torn into pieces	8 lettuce leaves, torn into pieces
salt	salt
1 tablespoon vinegar	1 tablespoon vinegar
1 tablespoon sugar	1 tablespoon sugar

Heat the oil in the wok. Add the garlic and fry for 1 minute. Add the cucumber and green pepper and stir-fry for another minute. Add the tomatoes and lettuce and stir-fry for a further minute. Mix in a little salt to taste, the vinegar and sugar. Stir-fry the ingredients for about 2 minutes or until the lettuce has wilted.
Serves 6

Tangy New Potato Salad

METRIC/IMPERIAL	AMERICAN
1 kg/2 lb small new potatoes, washed but not scraped	2 lb small new potatoes, washed but not scraped
5 tablespoons olive oil	5 tablespoons olive oil
3 tablespoons wine vinegar	3 tablespoons wine vinegar
2 teaspoons dry mustard	2 teaspoons dry mustard
2 tablespoons chopped parsley	2 tablespoons chopped parsley
salt and freshly ground pepper	salt and freshly ground pepper

Add enough water to the wok to come just below the steaming rack. Place the potatoes on the rack. Bring the water to the boil, then reduce to simmering point. Cover with the lid and steam the potatoes for about 20 minutes or until tender, depending on size. (Test them with a knife.)

Meanwhile, mix the oil, vinegar, mustard, parsley and salt and pepper to taste together in a serving bowl. Add the potatoes and gently toss until coated with the dressing. Serve hot or cold.
Serves 4

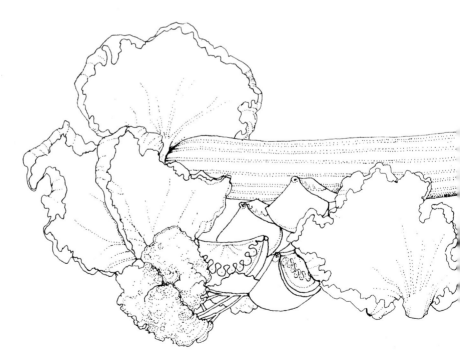

Piquant Stir-Fried Mushrooms

METRIC/IMPERIAL	AMERICAN
3 tablespoons oil	3 tablespoons oil
1 clove garlic	1 clove garlic
1 cm/½ inch piece root ginger	½ inch piece ginger root
1 leek, halved and thinly sliced	1 leek, halved and thinly sliced
225 g/8 oz button mushrooms, stalks removed	½ lb button mushrooms, stems removed
large pinch of sea salt	large pinch of coarse sea salt
large pinch of toasted sesame seeds	large pinch of toasted sesame seeds
1 teaspoon soy sauce	1 teaspoon soy sauce

Heat the oil in the wok with the clove of garlic and piece of ginger. Cook for 1 to 2 minutes, stirring occasionally. Remove the garlic and ginger. Add the leek and stir-fry for 2 minutes. Add the mushrooms and stir-fry for a further 2 minutes. Add the sea salt and half the sesame seeds. Sprinkle over the soy sauce and toss all the ingredients together for about 1 minute. Sprinkle over the remaining sesame seeds and serve on a bed of cooked noodles.
Serves 3

French (Green) Beans and Tomatoes

METRIC/IMPERIAL	AMERICAN
2 tablespoons oil	2 tablespoons oil
1 clove garlic	1 clove garlic
450 g/1 lb French beans, trimmed	1 lb green beans, trimmed
salt and freshly ground pepper	salt and freshly ground pepper
4 tablespoons water	¼ cup water
4 tomatoes, skinned and chopped	4 tomatoes, peeled and chopped
2 tablespoons chopped parsley	2 tablespoons chopped parsley

Heat the oil and garlic in the wok. Add the beans and stir-fry for 2 minutes. Sprinkle with salt and pepper to taste and pour in the water. Cover with the lid and cook for 8 minutes, stirring occasionally. Remove the clove of garlic and add the tomatoes. Cook, uncovered, for a further 5 minutes. Stir in the parsley and serve.
Serves 4

Courgettes (Zucchini) with Cream and Almonds

METRIC/IMPERIAL
salt and freshly
  ground pepper
2 tablespoons flour
450 g/1 lb courgettes,
  cut into 1 cm/
  ½ inch slices
25 g/1 oz butter
2 tablespoons oil
50 g/2 oz blanched
  almonds
150 ml/¼ pint soured
  cream

AMERICAN
salt and freshly
  ground pepper
2 tablespoons flour
1 lb zucchini, cut into
  ½ inch slices
2 tablespoons butter
2 tablespoons oil
½ cup blanched
  almonds
⅔ cup sour cream

Season the flour with salt and pepper and use to coat the courgettes (zucchini). Heat the butter and oil in the wok. Add the courgettes (zucchini) and stir-fry until browned on both sides. Push to one side. Add the almonds to the wok and fry for about 5 minutes or until golden. Stir the cream into the courgettes (zucchini) and almonds. Heat through, adding salt and pepper if necessary.
Serves 4

Lettuce Parcels

METRIC/IMPERIAL
2 tablespoons oil
3 slices pickled or
  peeled root ginger,
  finely chopped
1 green pepper,
  seeded and
  shredded
1 jar bean sprouts,
  drained
1 teaspoon salt
pinch of sugar
8 large crisp lettuce
  leaves

AMERICAN
2 tablespoons oil
3 slices pickled ginger
  or peeled ginger
  root, finely chopped
1 green pepper,
  seeded and
  shredded
1 jar or can (4-6 oz)
  bean sprouts,
  drained
1 teaspoon salt
pinch of sugar
8 large crisp lettuce
  leaves

Heat the oil in the wok. Add the ginger and green pepper and stir-fry for a few seconds. Add the bean sprouts, salt and sugar and stir-fry for 1 to 2 minutes. Place a spoonful of this mixture in the centre of each lettuce leaf and fold into a parcel.
Serves 4

Hot Tossed Salad

METRIC/IMPERIAL
1 Cos lettuce
2 teaspoons pure
  sesame oil
2 tablespoons oil
1 jar Chinese
  vegetables
½ medium red
  pepper, cored,
  seeded and sliced
1 tablespoon light soy
  sauce
1 tablespoon
  barbecue sauce
1 tablespoon good
  quality oyster sauce
1 teaspoon sugar

AMERICAN
1 head Romaine
  lettuce
2 teaspoons pure
  sesame oil
2 tablespoons oil
1 jar Chinese
  vegetables
½ medium-size red
  pepper, seeded and
  sliced
1 tablespoon light soy
  sauce
1 tablespoon
  barbecue sauce
1 tablespoon good
  quality oyster sauce
1 teaspoon sugar

Tear the lettuce into individual leaves and cut each leaf into quarters. Heat the oils in the wok. Add the Chinese vegetables and red pepper and stir-fry for 1 minute. Add the lettuce, soy sauce, barbecue sauce, oyster sauce and sugar. Toss all the ingredients together for 1 minute.
Serves 4
Illustrated on page 14

Index

The publishers wish to acknowledge the following photographers –
Robert Golden: pages 19; 46; 54 and 59; Eric Carter: page 38.
Illustrations by Susan Neale.